JOURNEY TO
JERUSALEM

GRACE HALSELL
JOURNEY TO JERUSALEM

Macmillan Publishing Co., Inc.

NEW YORK

Macmillan Publishing Co., Inc.
866 Third Avenue, New York, N.Y. 10022
Collier Macmillan Canada, Ltd.

Library of Congress Cataloging in Publication Data

Halsell, Grace.
    Journey to Jerusalem.

    1. Israel—Description and travel.   2. Jordan
(Territory under Israeli occupation, 1967-   )—De-
scription and travel.   3. Jewish-Arab relations.
4. Halsell, Grace.   5. Journalists—Texas—Biography.
I. Title.
DS107.4.H26   956.94′05   80-39649
ISBN 0-02-547590-8

10 9 8 7 6 5 4 3 2 1

Designed by Jack Meserole

Printed in the United States of America

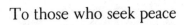

To those who seek peace

Contents

JOURNEY TO
JERUSALEM

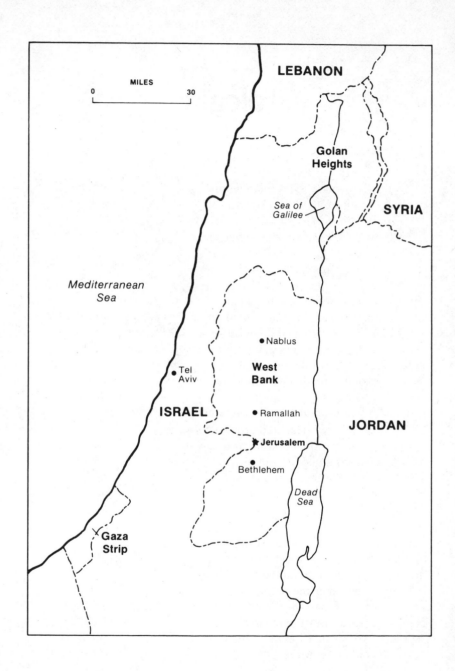

Prologue

Nahla is a young Palestinian woman in a refugee camp. One day, as I stood with her and her friends, I saw them throw stones at passing cars driven by Jewish settlers such as Linda and Bobby, native-born New Yorkers who have settled on the West Bank—the land of the Palestinians.

I have been on the side of Bobby and Linda, their side, so to speak, because I was accepted into their home and slept in one of their beds, wondering if Palestinians, armed with more than stones, might attack us and, in such a shoot-out, I know that the Palestinians would kill me as well as the Jewish settlers.

On another occasion, as I am strolling with several women students on the Palestinian Bir Zeit University campus near the West Bank town of Ramallah, I suddenly see uniformed Israeli soldiers running toward us. They are throwing tear gas, officers are shouting orders in Hebrew, and soldiers are firing rifles into the air—and their shots whiz over my head and around my ears.

I turn to flee in the opposite direction, but the soldiers are behind as well as in front and around us. I see that three have pinned Ghassan, a student I know, to the ground, and one is beating his stomach and face with the butt of a rifle, and blood is pouring from his face. Other soldiers, rushing past me, knock me to the ground, and I look up and into a face—a face of a soldier who in a moment of passion could kill me as well as Palestinians.

An officer, or one who is shouting commands to the others around us, seeing me pinned to the ground, the butt of a rifle in my face and the soldier momentarily hesitating to beat me—as the others are beating Ghassan—shouts to the man over me. I do not understand the words, but the meaning I gather from his quick motion to hair and eyes, is that I am not one of them, that I am a foreigner.

The soldier removes the butt of his rifle from my face, and I

1

scramble to my feet and try to run, but my knees collapse and I fall—
and again I see a soldier beating Ghassan, the blood still pouring
from his face. This is a somewhat typical day in the Occupied West
Bank.

I went to the Holy Land without knowing any one, and I began
to meet women and men who represent the three great religions that
came from a small desert region in the Middle East. These three
religions are monotheistic. They hold a belief not only in one God,
but a belief in the same God, the God of Abraham. Moreover, in all
of them Abraham represents not dogma, but a search for God, and
in searching for Him, finding the way to do His will, on earth and for
heaven.

In studying the holy words of Judaism, Christianity, and Islam,
one easily finds that in addition to a belief in one God they cherish
the same values, such as justice, mercy, and humility.

Because the three religions sprang from one small desert region,
the nearly one billion Christians and the eight hundred million Muslims and the fifteen million Jews all claim this small area of the world
as the heart-center of their faith.

Originally I had planned to write about three families representing the three faiths. And I thought to leave aside politics. I quickly
learned, however, that that would be like going to Antarctica and
not mentioning the ice. "Leave out politics!" exclaimed one resident.
"We *eat* politics morning, noon, and night."

The politics is all about land. Historic Palestine was small, about
the size of Vermont. I recall hearing the American interdenomina-
tional minister, Dr. Harry Emerson Fosdick, telling of his journeys
in Palestine and saying you could climb a mountain and "look all
over it." That was before it was cut in half. Now the three million
Israelis who control the land confront the three million Palestinians
who have lost control of it. And the peace of the world depends on
their finding ways to live as neighbors.

When I was growing up, the maps I saw had a vast area called
the Levant, and the big powers used the lands and the peoples of
this area as surrogates and pawns to protect their national interests.
The Middle East has served as a bridge between three continents,
Europe, Asia, and Africa, and the big powers have always wanted to

control it for its strategic value. Now that 60 percent of the world's oil reserves is located in the Middle East, the world powers view the area as the most strategic of all areas. Hence, the Arab-Israeli conflict is of worldwide significance. And that conflict concerns the West Bank.

I went to the Holy Land without understanding exactly what or where the West Bank is, and I immediately bought a map. I found the Israeli cities and I saw the towns of the West Bank printed on this map, but I could not see any borders separating the land of the Palestinians from the land of the Israelis. Then I noted that the map was printed in Israel. I bought other maps printed in Israel and all showed the West Bank as part of Israel.

The Palestinians say they've been pushed into an area that is only one-quarter of the former Palestine, and that they want the Israeli occupying forces to leave, so that they can create a new Palestine.

The Israelis have the fourth- or fifth-largest fighting force in the world, while the Palestinians in the West Bank do not have guns or an army of any kind. What they call their freedom fighters and what others have called Palestinian terrorists operate out of the neighboring country of Lebanon.

In moving between Israel and the West Bank, one constantly sees sharp contrasts. The Israelis have one of the highest standards of living in the Middle East and they are advanced technologically. The Palestinians are not developed technologically and remain essentially a rural people. Yet culturally and educationally they are at a remarkable stage of development, on a par with any peoples of the Middle East.

I lived constantly with the tension one feels in any war zone. I felt the tension of the Israelis who are in control of the Palestinians and I felt the tension of the Palestinians who are under the gun. I was thrilled to be living in the land of Moses and Christ and Muhammad, but politics is the reality and at every hand I saw distrust and a fear of the future. I met only two or three people who laughed spontaneously and naturally, simply to express a joy in life. Celebrations center around war and God. All of life is very real and earnest. The suffering, past or present, is up close.

Three women I met seem to pose three questions, and these questions will need to be addressed in any future peace settlement.

I stayed for a time in a refugee camp with a young Arab Muslim named Nahla, who poses the question, Where is the Palestine for the Palestinians? And I stayed awhile with an Arab Christian family whose youngest member, named Mervat, poses the question, Will Christians continue to leave the land of Christ? And I stayed awhile with Linda and her husband Bobby, natives of New York, who, armed with submachine guns, staked out a colony on West Bank Arab land. They vow that keeping the West Bank under Israeli control is more important than peace.

Nahla, Mervat, Linda—these three and the many other Jews, Christians, and Muslims I came to know have a history, a story, a struggle, a hope. You, perhaps, will identify with each, as did I.

JUDAISM
CHRISTIANITY
ISLAM

With Israelis in Jerusalem

On my first visit, I flew into Tel Aviv without a reservation. Checking at the airport tourist office, I learn I can get a room at the Ariel Hotel in Jerusalem. After clearing customs, I carry my bag to a Mercedes taxi and travel with six other passengers into West Jerusalem.

At the Ariel Hotel—it is now about midnight—I am led to a suite. Exhausted from the long flight, I decide to sleep and ask the price later.

The next morning I go to the office of the manager, Raoul R. Kohen, who, I learn, is from Egypt. He formerly worked as an assistant manager of the King David Hotel, and while there met a young American named Patricia, who was Roman Catholic, and had come to Jerusalem on vacation. They fell in love and in order to marry—in Israel a Jew can marry only another Jew—she converted to Judaism.

In our pleasant conversation I mention the magnificent view of the Old City from my window. "Leon Uris wrote a portion of *Exodus* in this hotel," Kohen relates. "The Israeli government had provided him free living quarters in a beautiful artists' colony, but he wanted to move here. He liked it—because of the view."

As nice as the view might be, I say I can't afford a suite.

"Stay for a few days at the price of a regular room—thirty-three dollars. And enjoy the view," he suggests.

I think that's a good idea.

I often walk to the King David Hotel. One day, I stand on the hotel terrace chatting with a new acquaintance. He is in his late thirties, with a beard. He is wiry, alert, polite, efficient at his job. I know this, because a few days before I had opened a checking account in the King David branch of Bank Leumi, where he works. His name, I learn, is Benjamin Esaguy Doukarsky.

"I was born in Brazil. My father was Portuguese and my mother was from Russia. My father was Sephardic and my mother Ashkenazic."

So what is he?

"I do not know," he smiles.

Does he go to the synagogue?

"Only once a year, only for something special."

Does he want to teach his children the Jewish religion? "Not the religion. But the traditions, so they will know their roots. They have not as yet started to school. When they do, I will not object to their studying the Bible. The Bible," he adds, "is part history, part archaeology—a little of everything."

Soon after opening an account, I need to add more to it, so I wire home for money. It does not arrive at the King David branch, so I go to the main Leumi office. I sit in front of the desk of M. Laufer, a vice-manager, and observe his talking on four phones, his constant assault by a stream of persons wanting his decision or a signature on paper. I am one of those besieging him, giving him a portion of my emotional stress. I want to send out a different signal, so, when he motions for me to tell him my problem, I ask: Where was he born?

"Rumania," he replies, relaxing and eager to relate his history. He came to Israel in 1955, when he was thirty-five. And he learned Hebrew. And so we talk. But eventually, hearing my money is not there, I stand up to leave. He does not want me to go. Like most busy people, he will take the time to talk about what is really important to him—where he was born and how it was growing up.

Several months later, on a bitter cold day with rainy, slippery streets, I am again walking near the central Bank Leumi. I see a man in front of me slide, and fall ingloriously into a shapeless heap. I run to his side, alarmed that he may be hurt. He looks like the banker, M. Laufer. The man is speaking, in English, as though to himself: "What can you do?"

Shaken, physically and emotionally, he gets to his feet. I hold on to him, wondering what can I do? Impulsively, I take his face in my hands and I kiss his cheek. I tell him I love him. Then, certain he is steady on his feet, I leave. I know he is not the banker. He is any man.

One evening I am invited to the home of one of Israel's leading publishers, Emanuel Hausman, who runs Carta Publishing Company. He calls for me at St. Andrew's Guest House, a part of the imposingly beautiful Church of Scotland built during the British mandate of Palestine. The Guest House, like the Ariel Hotel, also has a spectacular view of the Old City, with rooms at half the price. Hausman and I drive to a section of Jerusalem called the German district. Momentarily I feel I might be in Frankfurt or Berlin. When I enter his home I meet his wife, Charlotte, who leads me to a parlor decorated in quiet good taste with shelves of books, paintings, and a few artistically arranged flowers on a low, square coffee table.

Hausman, I learn, was born in Germany. The Nazis imprisoned his parents and both died in a concentration camp. Charlotte was born in Czechoslovakia. Her parents also were in a concentration camp but managed to survive.

"We came here before Israel's independence, when England had its mandate," Charlotte relates. "Emanuel served in the British forces for three years and was sent to Italy during World War II. I also served—as a nurse—in the British forces. And I was sent to Italy, where we met, fell in love, and were married."

Charlotte serves a French-style apple tart she has baked, and she and her husband talk to me about their children. A daughter is married to an Israeli, they have three children, and live in California; a son is in New York. Only a seventeen-year-old daughter, Delphne, is at home. She is sequestered in her room with her boyfriend, a soldier.

"They've been in that room a long time," her father comments.

"Now, remember how you were at that age," her mother reasons.

A door opens and an extremely tall young woman, and her soldier friend, enter the room. Delphne asks her father for money, which he gives her. Then she and the soldier leave.

"Teenagers are liberated regarding money," Hausman says, adding that for movies or meals, "sometimes the man but often the woman pays."

"It's only right," Charlotte believes. "Soldiers have so little money." (A private's pay is three hundred dollars a month.)

Every Israeli Jew—with a few exceptions for religious reasons—must begin duty at eighteen and serve for three years. Those who aspire to become an officer serve four years. "You are always on reserve, and, no matter who you are, you must serve one month out of every year until fifty-five," Hausman tells me.

Another evening I attend a cocktail party in the elegant home of a factory owner, Avner Peretz, and his wife Judy. The drinks flow as they do at cocktail parties back in Washington, D.C. I mention the drinks flowing because I have noticed the typical Israeli host, such as Hausman, does not offer a guest a cocktail, but rather tea or coffee. In this respect, many Jews are like the Arabs—Arab Muslims and Arab Christians—who drink little, if at all.

In inviting me, Peretz had promised, "You'll meet everybody who is anybody," and once he had the president of Israel, Yitzhak Navon, and Mayor Teddy Kollek in tow, he sidled up, saying, "See, didn't I tell you!"

At the party's end, new acquaintances who are driving me home ask if I had known Peretz long. No, not long, I say.

I had read an article in the English-language Jerusalem *Post* about his factory, called Pereg Metal Works, located in East Jerusalem. I became interested in knowing more about a Jewish-owned factory located in a sector of East Jerusalem that is inhabited by Arabs. I called and arranged to visit the factory.

At the factory in the Atarot Industrial Zone, I met Peretz, a personable man who is a third-generation Sephardic Jew from Spain. "My father and I started the factory in 1954. In that year we turned out eighty central heaters a month. Now we turn out fourteen thousand a month. We started with six workers; now we have two hundred, half of them Arab. Our employees work nine and a half hours a day, 5 days a week. They are off on Friday, the Muslim holy day, and on Saturday, the Jewish Sabbath. We pay a minimum wage of five fifty a day. And workers earn between $220 to $365 a month," Peretz said.

Amnon Angel, a bachelor in his thirties with even, attractive features, serves as production manager. He tells me he takes three vacations a year, usually on Jewish holidays. "I enjoy skiing in Austria, and I take long motor trips in America. Once I drove fourteen thousand miles and visited all the national parks in the United States. That vacation lasted two and a half months. I loved it. America is the cheapest country in the world to live in. Prices in the United States are lower than in Israel, and salaries are higher."

After meeting Israel's President Navon at the cocktail party in the Peretz home, I saw him again at a reception given for two hundred major donors to the United Jewish Appeal. President Navon dispensed with the familiar speech, thanking generous Americans for their contributions—and asked them to move to Israel.

"We are grateful [for your money]. But to be frank, I must say that what Israel needs more than any other thing is *aliya*—that is, people. Come with your money or without your money. It's high time for Jews in New York not to be surprised when they hear this demand."

The president's remarks did not receive an enthusiastic ovation. After Navon left, one New Yorker turned to a friend and said, "Why don't they worry first about all the Israelis living in New York?"

About ten thousand Israelis immigrate to the United States each year, while only three thousand Americans immigrate to Israel. Government statisticians say this imbalance in the population movement between the two main Jewish centers in the world today is one of the graver aspects of Israel's emigration problem.

Another day, I am invited for tea in the home of Eliahu and Zehava Elath. I relish sitting in their tastefully decorated home, among their paintings and art objects. Elath is one of the men who brought about the creation of Israel. "I moved to Washington and set up offices in the early nineteen forties," he tells me. He is writing his memoirs and brings me Volume One, which falls open to a full-page photograph of a presidential adviser, Clark Clifford. "He helped us tremendously," Elath says. Next I see a full-page picture of President Truman. Elath and others influenced Clifford, who in turn influenced Truman to support the creation of a Jewish state.

All such momentous events in history! And all happening within the lifetime of so many of us.

Arab Jews:
The Silent Majority

Once in New York, before going to Jerusalem, I saw a documentary film entitled *We Are Arab Jews in Israel.* Igaal Niddam, the producer-director, himself an Arab Jew, examines the lives of Jews of color who live in a state that is run by white, Western Jews.

Seeing the film, I learned for the first time that in Israel, Arab or Oriental Jews are the majority. I had presumed the Ashkenazim to be the majority. Most Jews in America are Ashkenazim. Their forebears came from Germany (and other Eastern European countries) and also from Russia.

Arab Jews are indigenous to the Mediterranean area that traditionally has been the land of the Arabs, including Syria, Lebanon, Morocco, Algeria, Libya, Iran, Iraq, historic Palestine, as well as Spain, which for eight hundred years was ruled by Arabs.

In his film Niddam tells us that the terms Oriental and Sephardic are used interchangeably to indicate an Arab Jew. He shows scenes of Arab Jews in Israel playing Arabic music on Arabic instruments and speaking to one another in Arabic.

In the film we come to know a variety of men and women from many lands around the Mediterranean who have settled in historic Palestine. And Niddam is telling us, "We are all Arab Jews living in Israel, and we are the majority of the Jews in Israel. Arab Jews now represent sixty-five percent of the population of Israel. Yet, no one knows about us."

The film makes extensive use of interviews with Eli Eliachar, a former member of the Israeli parliament (Knesset) and a leader for three decades of the Sephardic community in Jerusalem. One day, after I telephone and make an appointment to visit him, his wife receives me in their elegant home and graciously serves tea and cake.

12

Then she leaves me to talk with her husband in his book-lined study. Eliachar, tall, zestful, and appearing about twenty years younger than his age—somewhere in his eighties—begins to talk.

"My forebears for centuries lived in Spain. And for hundreds of years, the Jews and Muslims lived together there in peace. The philosopher Maimonides, who was born in Cordova, Spain, was one of the best known of the Sephardic Jews. He contrived the vast synthesis of Aristotelian philosophy and Jewish theology. Maimonides knew all the sciences of his time, and he possessed a special affection for astronomy. He also was a medical doctor and personal physician to the Arab ruler, Saladin.

"My forebears left Spain in 1492, the year the Jews were expelled from Spain," Eliacher continues, adding, "You recall it was the Christians, not the Muslims, who expelled the Jews.

"For centuries the Sephardim wandered far and wide within the Arab world, from Spain and Egypt to Turkey and beyond. We take pride in our tradition of learning. Sephardic Jews have always served as advisers, educators, administrators. Also, the Sephardic Jews, regardless of where they lived, kept alive the spiritual and cultural values of Judaism.

"After Israel was created, the doors were opened to Jews from all over the world, and the Sephardim were most anxious to come. Many, like my family and others who have been here for generations, became well established. But the Orientals coming here in recent decades are for the most part very poor and have little formal education. Because of their poverty, poor education, and darker skin, most Oriental Jews have been relegated to second-class citizenship. They have been given only a token participation in the direction of Israel's destiny. Only a few act as representatives in the parliament; only a few make it to lower-level ministerial posts.

"The gap between Oriental Sephardim and Western or European Jews in housing, education, and jobs is widening."

To make his point, Eliachar draws a large, rectangular box covering the lower half of a page. "The Palestinian Arabs living in Israel, Gaza, and the West Bank are there." He draws another large box, "And the Israeli Oriental Jews are there." Then he draws a smaller box, "for the Israeli Ashkenazim," and he places a minuscule box on top, for the ruling Ashkenazim. "The big money from America pours into a minuscule group of ruling Ashkenazim, and they keep it for their kind.

"Jews from East-Central Europe represent the origin of the complex political party system that governs Israel," he continues. "Their political parties are still dependent on the Zionist organization for their financial requirements. The European Ashkenazim have retained control of all branches of government. The Orientals do not have proper representation in either legislative or executive branches, and, because they do not have proper representation, they do not succeed in having their problems seriously considered. The Ashkenazim establishment holds full power in every respect.

"With only European Jews in control, Israeli democracy is a mere caricature. The rich are getting richer; the poor getting poorer. Because of this widening gap, poverty, delinquency, lack of equal opportunities in education and advancement cause eruption of popular anger, such as the Israeli Black Panther protest movement of the Sephardim," Eliachar says.

"It is a new thing when the Israeli army must fight other Israelis. You hear the Jewish masses of Tel Aviv talking exactly like the Palestinian Arabs, and they are taking tires and burning them in the center of Tel Aviv to demonstrate against inequality. And this is more dangerous to our state than when the Palestinian Arabs do the same thing in Nablus or Ramallah."

I had seen several of the Sephardic protest demonstrations. Once in Tel Aviv I watched about one thousand slum-dwellers in Kfar Shalem block a highway with a barrage of burning tires. At the same moment, residents of two other neighboring slums blocked other highways. They thus cut off Israel's largest city from half the country, and for more than three hours police battled the demonstrators— Oriental Jews—who shouted, "We want better housing."

And in Jerusalem, one day after prices of milk, bread, and other staples soared by 120 percent, slum-dwellers—almost all Arab Jews—took to the streets, stoning cars, upsetting and burning police cars, wounding police officers, and shouting, "Fight poverty! Don't waste money on (West Bank) settlements." But despite their protests against such expenditures, the Begin government announced new settlements.

"Nations often destroy themselves by refusal to deal with problems at home," Eliachar warns. "Israel's refusal to give equality to the Sephardim is the biggest problem we face. Our racism at home is a bigger problem than the enemy without. Since the creation of Israel, I repeatedly have warned that white Europeans who assume leadership must not practice racism and must accept dark-skinned Arab Jews as equals.

"The continued relegation of Sephardim to second-class citizenship is no longer a communal problem. It is Israel's responsibility to prevent a further deepening of the rift between Sephardim and Ashkenazim that endangers the unity of our people and Israel's survival. I do not believe acculturation or a melting into the pot is the answer for the Sephardim," he continues, pointing out that differences enrich a culture. "I want a recognition of the differences and a utilization of all that the Sephardim can offer the society at large.

"The Sephardic Jews, speaking Arabic and understanding Arabs, could build a bridge between the Jews and Arab Muslims and Arab Christians. Many Sephardim are experts on Arabic languages and literature; many are distinguished scholars. And they are not being used. As an example, not one Sephardi was asked to be a part of the peace negotiations before, during, or after the Camp David peace talks. Then, look at the appointment of Israel's first ambassador to Egypt.

"The Israeli government would not send an Israeli ambassador to Washington who did not speak English. Yet, our government sent to Egypt an ambassador who does not speak Arabic. Not only does the Israeli so named, Eliahu Ben Elissar, not know Arabic, but also he does not have any close contacts with Arabs of any class. As he does not know their psychology and peculiarities, he cannot predict their reactions. He will therefore have to depend on subalterns to keep him informed.

"The appointment, I believe, was an insult not only to Egypt, but also to every Sephardi. The Israeli government, run by European Jews, continues to ignore the fact that the majority of the Jewish population of Israel comes from Arab countries."

Although the Orientals have until now seen the Arabs around them as their enemy, one day, Eliachar warns, the Sephardic Jews, having known only discrimination from the white European Jews who, from its inception, have run Israel, "may decide they have more in common with the Arabs—and make common cause with them."

Eliachar, well aware of his rich heritage, can proudly say he is an Arab Jew, but I met many Oriental-Sephardic-Arab Jews who would like to "pass" for a white, European Ashkenazi. Because they look like the enemy, they try to put a distance between themselves and the enemy. So they say they hate—even more than the Western Jews say they hate—the enemy, the Arab.

I knew of several examples of Oriental Jews who, although having the same pigmentation and features of Arabs, indicated a hatred of them. Once, walking near the King David Hotel, an Oriental Jew—I guessed him to be from Iraq or Algeria or Morocco—came alongside me and began a conversation. We walked for a few blocks and suddenly he said with vehemence, "I hate Arabs. They are dirty. They smell bad." Apparently he needed to reassure himself that he was not at all the same as the enemy.

Once Jacques, an immigrant Sephardic Jew from Morocco, drove me in his car from Jewish West Jerusalem to Arab East Jerusalem. At St. Stephen's Gate, we asked directions to a certain convent. In replying, an Arab youngster spoke to me in English, but then, seeing the dark-skinned Jacques at the wheel, switched to Arabic.

As we drove off, Jacques said bitterly, "He thinks I am one of *them.*"

Jacques, feeling himself a second-class citizen, desperately needed, it seemed to me, to reassure himself he is not a man of color in a society of white rulers.

On another day, a tall, dark-skinned man, about thirty-five, approaches me, introduces himself as Joseph, and, after we chat for a few moments, he volunteers, "I come from Russia."

Russia? I ask, adding that he looks Oriental or Sephardic. Some while later, he admits he is not from Russia but from Iraq. He says he tells strangers he is from Russia so "they will like me better."

Going to
the Synagogues

With almost every Jewish community in the world represented, Israel has more than six thousand different synagogues. I have been to several, the first being a Sephardic synagogue. Altogether there are eighty-eight sects of Jews, and the majority—about fifty—belong to the Sephardim.

In the Jerusalem Sephardic synagogue I attended, members are direct descendants of the Jews forced to leave Spain during the Inquisition. Some of the chants and melodies used in their prayers are the same as those of their forefathers in Spain four and a half centuries ago. Instead of a rabbi they have a "wise man," and their synagogue is not only a place of worship but a kind of community center as well. "We are a big family helping one another," one Sephardi told me.

As Eliachar pointed out, the Jews who were expelled from Spain went to Turkey, and then after the Turkish conquest, began to arrive in Jerusalem. They set about constructing synagogues and built four Sephardic synagogues on the ruins of an old Crusader church. The complex—known as the Ben Zakkai Synagogue—became the center of the Sephardic community.

Jerusalem synagogues often reveal architectural origins, particularly the one called the Istanbul Synagogue, which is reminiscent of certain buildings in Turkey. The Eliahu Hanavi Synagogue, built in the same style as the Istanbul, has preserved certain traditional relics, such as the chair Elijah the Prophet allegedly sat in. It is displayed on a wall.

Other than the Turkish influence, one finds few distinctive forms of synagogue architecture in West or New Jerusalem. The builders, all constructing their edifices in the past decades, made use of local materials, including eucalyptus, olive wood, and Jerusalem stone. The menorah used on the exterior epitomizes the light of the Torah; it also is an emblem of the state of Israel. The Hadassah Medical Center Synagogue, containing Marc Chagall's world-famous stained-glass windows, attracts the most tourists.

A partition between the main hall and a small women's gallery or *mehizah*, prevails in all, with variation as to the form and height of the latticed wall, window, or curtain separating the women. I found one exception to this separation: the Hebrew University Synagogue is the only one where men and women may worship together.

Traditionally, in almost all synagogues, the platform, or *bimah*, is situated in the middle of the synagogue. The precentor's lectern, or *ammud*, is close to the Ark of the Covenant, with the scrolls of the Torah at the front wall.

Orthodox Judaism, to all intents and purposes, is the "established church" of the state. Religious law, or the *halacha*, is state law in all matters affecting personal status, which includes marriage, divorce, legitimacy, and conversion, with the rabbinical court having the status of civil courts of law.

Both Sephardic and Ashkenazic Jews have their chief rabbis, and they often disagree on the most crucial of issues. For instance, Sephardic Chief Rabbi Ovadia Yosef insists that the *halacha* permits—even requires—Jews to relinquish parts of militarily controlled Palestinian Arab lands if doing so is likely to save lives. Ashkenazic Chief Rabbi Shlomo Goren opposes relinquishing Palestinian Arab territory now under Israeli military rule.

In 1948, Israel became a Jewish state, founded largely by practicing socialists who were nonpracticing Jews. "Most of Israel's independence heroes," explains one orthodox rabbi, "were people who deeply valued Jewish tradition but also wanted to build a fundamentally secular state—where religion would have a respected place on the sidelines."

The rigidly religious community, represented by the National Religious Party (NRP) has held seats in all governments since Israel's birth, influencing all of them, threatening more than a few, and toppling one. Religious zealots are a minority with power far beyond their numbers in a country where fewer than one in three persons is an orthodox or traditional Jew.

David Ben-Gurion, Israel's first prime minister, wanted to round up the Jews from all corners of the earth and bring them "home" to Palestine, and so he said to the Yemenite Jews, "Come home to Israel." They did not know it was a place on a map. Israel, Zion, Jerusalem—all were names for some celestial paradise. They thought it was prophesy that wings were provided to get them there.

The United States Air Force cooperated by providing waves of "magic carpets"—transporting sixty-five thousand Yemenite Jews from their desert homes to Israel. Flight crews recall how amazed they were to find the Yemenites camping in the aisles, lighting fires to brew their tea. Even aboard the plane, they carried on their desert way of life, setting up portable altars, tending to their children and animals. An ancient, mystic aura seemed to surround them.

This ancient, mystic aura prevails in a "living museum" or Yemenite synagogue. Sitting in a small reserved cubicle for women, I watch the old men—keepers of the letter of the word, many in their eighties and nineties, with long beards and biblical faces. They swing and sway, and, as in a Navajo healing ceremony, I feel transported back a thousand years in time.

"The Jewish Yemenites are a desert people who lived in isolation for a couple of thousand years," a rabbi explained. "It is said they could not ride donkeys or camels, being 'poor Jews,' so that in their prayers they developed a vigorous rocking or swaying motion that is combined with their desert cry." Their chants or cries seem to come from a faraway place that is all sand and sky and loneliness. It comes from some source such as wild winds and is haunting and piercing— a sound that was here before men turned their mouths to making words.

On entering the synagogue's small niche for women, I step in front of four old women, very wrinkled, and ease myself alongside three very young women, none yet twenty. The young Yemenite women are noted for their smooth olive skin and their large, dark, strikingly beautiful—and mysterious—eyes. One has long hair, and another next to me has short hair, stylishly combed. One old woman is saying—so I am able to gather from her gestures—that I should have a kerchief over my head, and the young women are saying, oh, let her alone. We all peer from time to time into the main hall to see what the men are doing, as the women must follow their lead as to when to sit or stand and what prayers to say or sing. One of the young girls shares her prayer book. She forces it into my hands, and indicates she does not need to see it. I recall the legend that Yemenite Jews can read a book from all angles—from the left, right, and upside down, as well as right side up, their cleverness in this feat dating back to the time when prayer books, all written by hand, were very scarce, and one prayer book had to be shared and read by a group of worshipers at the same time. What originally was a necessity caused by the shortage of print developed later into custom.

As the women chant, I mouth words to a hymn I know, and the women do not notice or, if they notice, they do not care that my sounds are not in Hebrew.

Some men come to the synagogues with three to four wives. Polygamy, of course, is not practiced in Israel, but if Yemenis had the wives when they immigrated, no one interferes with their status quo.

A few men wear white turbans, white robes, and white stockings. They take off their shoes—as Muslims at a mosque—on entering the synagogue. "When Moses faced the Lord, he took off his shoes," an old Yemeni explains. Also, until 1979, they had another Muslim custom: the Yemenis prayed on the floor.

"Let's get some chairs in here," young Israelis repeatedly insisted.

"How can we be slaves of the desert and sit on chairs?" the old Yemenis asked. The young men insisted the old men must get off the floor. Then the old men made benches of stone so that "our worship will not be soft." The visitor detects few young Israelis in such synagogues, although one or two of the ancient Yemenis had a grandchild or great-grandchild with him.

I also went to a Persian synagogue, whose members are descendants of the Jewish community in a town in Persia where they had been influenced by Muslim culture. The Jews thus introduced into their synagogues a number of decorations, services, and ceremonies identical to those in the mosques. When these Jews immigrated from Persia to Jerusalem, they retained some of these customs; for instance, they chant exactly as in a mosque, except that the words are in Hebrew. Also, old men in this synagogue, as in the Yemenite synagogue, have the custom of taking off their shoes. A few of these Persian Jews retain a double first name—Jewish and Muslim. One finds names such as Abraham Abdualla Cohen.

The late head of this congregation was not called a rabbi, or *chacham*, but, a *hajji*, the title given to a devout Muslim who has been to Mecca. Instead of sitting facing the east next to the Holy Ark, as is customary in other synagogues, the *hajji*, or rabbi, sits near the entrance of the synagogue, a carryover no doubt from the time when the Jews had to be on guard against strangers entering the synagogue. On the Sabbath and on holy days the members of this congregation don black astrakhan hats, the headdress of the former Persian shah and Persian aristocracy. Again, borrowing from the Muslims, they make decorative use of the color green—the Islamic holy color—on all festive occasions, such as at a wedding, a *bar mitzvah*, the coming of age of a young man; and a circumcision, or *brith milah*.

Since almost all the Jews in the United States are Ashkenazim, and I had previously attended only Ashkenazic synagogues, it was perhaps only natural that when I went to a Jerusalem Ashkenazic synagogue I would feel at home. Again, I climb up to a loft that separates the women from the men. I immediately notice the blond hair and blue eyes of several of the women around me. Also I hear Western music with which I can easily identify. There is a curtain over a lattice window that separates us from the men, but the curtain has been tossed over the top of the lattice so that I can see the men in the main hall better than in the other synagogues. A woman next to me gives me an opened prayer book. The women, many with babes in arms, all easily accept me. I do not feel a stranger among them.

On another Friday, I go to a service at a Hasidic synagogue. Hasidism, a mystical, pietistic movement, derives its name from a Polish Jew who was born in the eighteenth century and given a place of honor in the twentieth century by the Jewish philosopher, Martin Buber.

Entering the synagogue, I climb steps to a loft and seat myself among four women, all with scarfs. Their religion dictates that they must shave their heads the night before they get married, and keep shaving it every twenty-eight days, the idea being that no man other than a husband will desire them. These women treat me as if I were unclean. They repeatedly point to my purse. I later learn that no Jew is allowed to carry anything to the synagogue on the Sabbath.

In their neighborhood they are most Orthodox. The men and boys, with long curls that dangle below their ears, have chalk-white faces from, one presumes, spending so much time indoors reading Holy Scripture. They wear black trousers and down-to-the-knees black coats and large fur hats—even in the searing Jerusalem summers—that their ancestors wore in the chilly climes of Poland, Russia, and Rumania.

Hasidic men are noted for their work in diamonds, cutting and shaping the stones. Israel, along with South Africa, Belgium, and New York, is one of the diamond centers of the world.

My interest in various synagogues led me to meet an Israeli, Joseph Hayardeni, forty-eight, who is a schoolteacher by profession but whose passion is his religion and its meaning to his nation. He conducts a Friday afternoon tour of synagogues, and when I went on one of his tours I was captivated by his dramatic ability and his zest—qualities a tour guide needs to keep sixty tourists awake on a scorching hot afternoon.

I ask Hayardeni if I might invite him for a coffee, and we fix a date and meet in the afternoon at the King David and sit on the terrace, but he does not order anything. "No, don't bother, I'm not thirsty," and he proceeds to tell me fascinating facts about the Jewish religion. We sit there, talking religion, for two hours. I say I wish I had brought my tape recorder. "Well, bring it next time," he suggests. "And come to my home for a Sabbath meal."

On the appointed Friday, I take a taxi to his very large and impressive home and find Hayardeni in his garden, inspecting pomegranates, figs, tomatoes, spices, and grapes. He leads me up steps and into his home and introduces me to his slender, attractive wife, who appears to be ten years younger than her husband, and to their children, a son and two daughters, and to his mother, who is in her eighties and speaks ten languages. I excuse myself and wash up, and we all sit down for the meal. I note the beautiful linen cloth and the candles and the silverware. Before Hayardeni breaks the hallowed bread, everyone gets up and washes his or her hands, so I again wash mine.

We are served two kinds of fish, a cod and a white fish, topped with a spicy sauce made with celery, garlic, tomatoes, and lemon slices. Then we are served boiled meatballs and two kinds of beef, fried and boiled. "A man works like a slave six days to live like a king on the Sabbath," Hayardeni explains. I note that Hayardeni is a modern, liberated man who helps his wife. He did all the shopping, and he made the sauce and cooked the fish and the meat, and he helps in the serving, all the while explaining himself and his family.

"The more religious the couple, the fewer the problems." And he adds, "If you give your children religious training as youngsters, they can then decide, on reaching maturity, whether they want less, more, or none."

How, I ask, did he and his wife meet? "We were in our twenties and went to dances, and he liked to dance the paso doble," his wife recalls. He was, she adds, "a good leader."

On another occasion I am invited to their home, and Mrs. Hayardeni prepares a lovely table of refreshments, featuring the seven best-known Israeli products, including crackers, representing wheat and corn, dates, pomegranates, figs, olives, grapes—almost all of these from their garden. She also serves a delicious white grape juice, and Hayardeni gives a certain toast to health, which, he says, should be used only with the juice of unfermented grapes.

From food and drink, Hayardeni turns the conversation to Judaism. He repeats his strong conviction that Jews, to retain their religion, must believe every word of their Holy Scripture. "We have a right to be here only if we are practicing the religion of Judaism. God will allow us to live here only if we are faithful to the Jewish religion and, if we lose our Judaism, we have no right to Israel." As for the Palestinian Arabs who were dispersed in 1948, "Jews would like to welcome them to return—but then we would become a minority, and if we are a minority, we are nothing. And we waited two thousand years to return to our land." He sees endless strife.

He believes the United States is turning its back on Israel "to get Arab oil. The only way that Israel would be free of its problems would be for the Arab nations not to have oil."

His reasoning—that the United States would not be interested in the Arabs if they did not have oil—of course may be right. I am inclined to believe it is. It may well be the pressure we get from oil-producing Arabs, such as the Saudis, who are telling us, the Palestinians are our brothers, that forces us to see those we have not seen.

On a Moshav
with Aviva and Reuven

I lived awhile with two couples, Aviva and Reuven within Israel proper, and with Jewish settlers Linda and Bobby in the Arab-inhabited West Bank. I found enormous differences in their idea of religion—one couple having a God of peace, and the other a God of war—and also in their idea of the boundaries of the state of Israel.

Aviva and Reuven think that the internationally recognized boundaries of Israel are fixed, and they do not want to risk war to extend those boundaries. Linda and Bobby say that war is not too big a price to pay for seizing more Arab land that will mean a Greater Israel.

I came to know Aviva and Reuven quite by accident. During the first days of my stay in the Holy Land, I signed for all available conducted tours, and on a tour of the Old City, among a group of tourists, I met Reuven. As everyone other than he and I arrived in pairs, we find ourselves walking side by side, listening to our young guide. Reuven, who is about forty-eight with fair skin and blue eyes, stands about five feet, five inches tall and is wearing shorts and a T-shirt. "I am a native of Rochester, New York, but I have lived in Israel since the time it became a state," he says.

Surely, I suggest, he must know the history of Israel better than the guide. And why, I ask, would he take a tour designed for newly arrived visitors?

"I'm a history buff," he replies.

The heat is oppressive and our group stops for cold drinks. Reuven speaks with several Americans about American baseball teams, the Orioles, Dodgers, and Yankees. Watching him, I understand his desire to stay in touch with his native soil, although, he tells me, he has not been back to America in three decades.

24

At the end of the tour we continue talking, and he invites me to visit him and his wife Aviva on a farm, or *moshav*, called Timoren, which is in the south, midway between Jerusalem and Beersheba. A few days later I telephone Aviva and immediately note her soft, appealing English accent. And like Reuven, she says yes, please come for a visit. On a day arranged, I take a bus and find myself knocking on a door; it opens and there stands Aviva.

She is wearing a simple flowered cotton dress and appears to be in her early forties, with short, casual, auburn hair beginning to turn gray. Of medium height, she stands straight, and comfortably carries a few extra pounds that give her an approachable, unsophisticated, natural look. She appears at ease with her role of housewife and keeper of a kitchen, one who always has a pot of coffee or a freshly baked pie or cake to offer her family and guests.

Seated in her living room, sipping coffee, I hear jets from a nearby Israeli airfield taking off. I presume they are on raids to South Lebanon, as the Israeli bombing there is intense at this time. Aviva and I begin to talk as if we had always known each other. She reveals herself as a woman reconciled with her life, knowing that she has, given the circumstances, done the best she could. She has a grown son, Danni, a grown stepson, Simon, and two children at home, Orly, thirteen, and Yuval, eight.

"I have always known war," she tells me, recalling she was a "war baby" in England. After she came to Israel she watched her first husband, then her present husband Reuven, her stepson Simon, then her son Danni—"all of them in uniform . . . always going off to a war, or to prepare for war.

"When Danni was four, I got down on my knees before him and prayed, 'Oh God, let there be no more wars.' And then when Yuval was born, I did not bother. I know he will go into uniform, that there will always be wars." The planes overhead drone ominously. One feels tension and the fear of war and destruction not only in Israeli cities but on Israeli farms as well.

Aviva makes no secret of the fear that permeates her life, the lives of the members of her family, and, she believes, the lives of almost all Israelis. She said she did not think the Arabs had a grasp of this all-pervasive fear until Egyptian President Sadat acknowledged that "the Jews have been living in fear for thousands of years," and that the Israelis saw themselves as "surrounded by millions of hostile Arabs."

She points out that if others, friends or enemies, would understand the often incomprehensible reactions Israelis make today, they must first of all understand that "we are governed by fear. It determines what we do or refrain from doing.

"We continue to re-live what happened to us in the past. So our fears do not lessen, but seem to grow. Even after thirty-two years of living in our own state, we have not escaped this feeling of fear. We feel we are surrounded by enemies on all sides."

At noon Aviva and I are seated at a small, round dining table and Yuval, her youngest child, comes in from school and joins us for lunch. Aviva and I continue to chat and eventually notice that Yuval is not eating but is turned in on himself, morose, withdrawn, sad— as if he is in another, horrible world, with dark clouds covering his handsome face.

"Yuval," asks Aviva, "why are you so sad?"

He sighs and with tears in his large eyes tells us about the Nazis killing children; he identifies with those children and he asks his mother, "Why do they hate me?" He breaks into tears over the Holocaust stories that are a mandatory subject in Israeli schools. Aviva puts her arms around Yuval and comforts him, reassuring him in the most tender, loving manner that she loves him, and I also put my arms around him, reassuring him that he is surrounded by love.

On another day, in another *moshav* home, a child came in from school weeping over the Holocaust stories she was taught in school. Her mother later tells me, "I think we are wrong, sowing insecurity, distrust, and hate. We are claiming that the Holocaust proved the whole world was against the Jews. This is not only bad psychology for our children, it's also historically wrong. If that were true, we wouldn't be here at all."

One day Reuven invites me for a tour of the grounds. As we stroll down a narrow paved road, I see look-alike houses and sprinklers spinning on look-alike lawns. For a moment I feel I am strolling near my mother's home in Fort Worth, Texas. Many *moshav* residents, like Aviva and Reuven, previously lived on a kibbutz, and as Reuven points out, "You live dormitory style on a kibbutz, but here you have a private home, and we preserve the traditional family unit. As you see, the homes are alike and that makes for some discord, even though we attempt to make democracy work. We give the same three-bedroom house to a newlywed couple and to a couple with eight children. Some may say that is equality and some, especially those with the large families, say it is not fair.

"The founding members were mostly from South Africa. Today, we have about three hundred people living here from the United States, Holland, Rumania, Brazil, Canada, Belgium, and Italy," Reuven says, adding that all but four of the *moshav* residents are Ashkenazim. The exceptions are a man and his wife from Egypt and another couple from Morocco.

"If a person has individual, personal goals, then I would say you've got to think twice before moving here. Because a work committee will decide that you will do this and that. Maybe you are needed in the dairy and maybe you don't like that work. You have a problem. You have to fit in where the community can fit you in. Sometimes it's what you like to do; sometimes it's what you least like to do. Now I feel you do what you have to do. Life is a series of compromises; it doesn't matter where you are."

At the dairy farm where Reuven himself works, tending and milking Holsteins, we stand outside a fenced enclosure. As he talks I realize he knows each cow not only by number but by name as well, and that for Reuven each has a distinct personality; one walks with a limp, another is good-natured, a third hard to please. Reuven shows me complex charts showing each cow's daily milk production and how these facts are fed into computers and how the computers tell him how to breed cow X with bull Z.

"In the beginning, Timoren was largely a farming community, but now young Israelis no longer want to do farm labor. Because we could no longer depend on agriculture alone, we had to diversify." As we continue our walk, Reuven shows me a small factory where the *moshav* residents produce plastic toys. We walk through another small factory where workers produce metal furniture. Workers also tend roses and carnations—grown in hothouses—for export. And they raise chickens for the sale of the fowls as well as the eggs.

With such activities, the *moshav* males earn money they put into community coffers. "We have a food allowance. Instead of this money going to a community kitchen, as in a kibbutz, we distribute it to families. A housewife gets a lump sum for running a house, and she manages the way she wants." The community also pays for tennis, volleyball, and basketball courts, as well as for a swimming pool. It picks up the tabs for all parties, movies, and holiday festivities.

On our walk, we pass a library and a clinic. "The community pays all health expenses," Reuven says. As I listen to the varied free attractions, I think the community sounds like a pattern for a workable welfare state. Reuven sees both sides.

"What are the needs of a person? Here, the individual does not decide. We, the community, decide the needs of a person. And not everybody thinks the same. We, the community, make decisions that in America are considered private or personal decisions. And because we live communally we experience a great deal of human friction. Almost any psychologist or psychiatrist will tell you that the closer you live in a community the greater the friction among individuals. And a visitor comes in from the outside and tells me, 'Well, how petty this is.' And he is right. We make decisions even about the smallest, most trivial matter. And we get into arguments. Therefore not everybody could live this way of life.

"It is difficult to attract and keep young people on the *moshav*," Reuven reiterates as we start toward home. As examples, he mentions his son Simon, and Aviva's son Danni. Both are now out of the army, but neither gives any indication he wants to settle down on the farm. Danni, for example, says he wants "to travel around the world."

"Life on the *moshav* for a single person can be dull," Aviva admits over supper that evening, "Here you are stuck at home. Youngsters want to get away from parents, and they should do it. It's not good to sit and live with your parents all your life. Danni has lots of opportunities; he is young."

Up to the age of thirty, Danni can apply to a *moshav* committee asking for the right to return. Obviously Aviva hopes he will do so. And, if the choice is between a stranger and a son, "we give priority to accepting a son," she adds.

I visit one day with a young, attractive career woman, Sonit Videvinsky, who left the *moshav* to live and work in Tel Aviv. Back on holiday to visit her parents, she talks about inflation. "An average two-bedroom apartment in Tel Aviv runs about five hundred dollars a month. You pay that much in New York, but the American pay scale is one-third higher than what we earn. Moreover, a Tel Aviv apartment, even at exorbitant prices, is almost impossible to find. For this reason, many young people put two and two together and they return to the *moshav*. Where else can a newlywed couple get a three-bedroom house simply for the asking?"

Shoshana, a Timoren resident, is to be married. Eighteen-and-a-half-years old, she served half a year in the army, and by getting married she will now be excused from army duty. Everyone in the *moshav* is getting ready for the wedding.

"If Shoshana lived in the United States, her mother would say, I want it this way. But a *moshav* wedding is different," Reuven explains. "The community as a whole makes the decisions. One wedding is not much different from another wedding because we want everybody to have approximately the same. And we can make a beautiful wedding."

"Everyone does something," Aviva adds. She displays a half-dozen mimeographed sheets of organized, detailed work procedures. One work team will bring tables and set them up. Aviva and a committee will arrange place settings. Older people fold napkins. Housewife X makes eggplant salad, Y makes potato salad, while Z arranges flowers. Reuven pinpoints his name. Sharply at 6:00 P.M., he—with a group of helpers—removes food from the community center refrigerators and places it on buffet tables. Another team, at a designated hour, will present a musical stage show.

At home, the Neuman's daughter, Orly, and I are dressing. She worries over what to wear—jeans or a dress—and eventually decides on the dress. We walk to the community center grounds, where about five hundred guests—from the bride's *moshav* and the bridegroom's *moshav*—are gathered. I note that Aviva, Orly, and I are among the few women wearing dresses, the majority being in jeans and blouses. It is a warm summer evening, and the men are not wearing coats or ties.

The bride, wearing an ankle-length beige dress and wedge shoes with strap ties, and the groom, in slacks with an open-neck shirt and a dazed, perpetual smile below his moustache, stand under a canopy held by two of Shoshana's brothers. A rabbi, checking his watch a couple of times, and determined, Aviva whispers, "to keep the ritual within ten minutes," performs a brief ceremony. Aaron Cohen, originally from Egypt, holds a bottle of red wine in his right hand and fills a glass, offering it to the rabbi, who smilingly rejects it. "No, fill it really full." Cohen fills it to overflowing and hands it to the rabbi, who in turn passes it to the couple, each taking a sip. The bride and groom are pronounced as one, and we move to the buffet tables and fill our plates with a rich variety of food.

The newlyweds will occupy one of the three-bedroom homes. He will work eight hours a day at a task on the *moshav*, and Shoshana will keep house. In this respect she will be no different from Aviva and all the women on the *moshav*. They were all housekeepers, so designated by the *moshav* constitution. "This ruling stipulating that women may have no meaningful work outside the home makes the *moshav* different from the kibbutz. In a kibbutz, the labor of the women, as well as that of the men, contributes to the community's coffers," Aviva explains.

One evening a neighbor, Mollye, originally from Washington, D.C., comes to visit. "We are breaking our heads on how to come to terms with the role of the woman. Many say they came here to be only housewives and they like the way it is now," Mollye tells me.

"*Moshav* rules specify a housewife should give a token four hours a week to some type of community duty, but some housewives complain about that," Aviva adds. "They like the easy life. They have these beautiful homes, and they like to go to coffee klatsches, and they like to live luxuriously. They say, why should I work myself to the bone? I can take all the benefits and not give anything. And the sad part is that the less work they do, the more they complain. And if the women are unhappy, the men also are discontented.

"The *moshav* has suffered two bad financial years, and I personally think we women have to get up and go out to work and earn money so that the *moshav* can supply us," Aviva continues. "The rule against women working has not been changed because we have something here—democracy, as it is called, and to change a rule we must hold a general meeting."

"Our general meetings are dominated by men with loud voices," Reuven explains. "Say you want to discuss the position of women. A man stands up and says, 'I think we should stick her next to the sink and next to the stove—and that is my opinion and my vote counts!'

This fight over the role of women has been going on for the twenty
years we've lived here," Reuven says.

"Things are changing," Mollye suggests, wanting to sound
optimistic.

"Mollye, you know the changes for women are slow," Reuven
reminds her.

"The problem has newer dimensions with our daughters returning home from college," Mollye points out. "We have gone to enormous expense and trouble to educate our children, and they come
back and say, what for? That is one of my daughter's questions. I
keep telling her not to study sociology. You won't be able to work as
a social worker at the *moshav*.

"I had to recognize that I, as a woman with too little to do, could
become frustrated and resentful of a husband's commitment to a
job," Aviva says. "At first, I got jealous of Reuven spending so much
time tending the cows. He would come in late and I would get mad
and say, oh go on back to the barns with your girlfriends. Then I
realized he stayed late because he had more work than he could han-
dle in eight hours. So I began helping him.

"I have my reasons for why I go to work in the barns: to help the
moshav and to help myself as well, so that I may develop and not be
a bored person all the time. Why shouldn't the other women also do
it? They will get the same benefits that I get. We all should work
and contribute because we chose to come here to a communal life."

As I visit with Aviva and Reuven and other couples in the
moshav, I repeatedly hear how they came to Israel to bend their
backs and how they relished hard work and long hours. The days
sped by because they shared a dream. One after the other they are
telling me that, "We had a spirit, a belief, a fervor, a zest, a conviction we were building not only for our own families but also for Jews
all over the world. We could work twelve hours, picking fruit, working in the fields. Everyone dressed simply, ate simply. We all had
our eyes on a common goal."

"Zionism for me was a socialist Zionism," Reuven explains. "I
grew up imbued with the historical idea of 'Hebrew labor' or 'the
conquest of labor' based on the populist agrarian socialist ideology of
A. D. Gordon, who, in the early twentieth century, preached the
redeeming force of physical labor. What did such a theory mean in

practical terms? It enabled us to believe that land bought from Arab absentee landlords provided not only the practical but also the moral basis for the young state of Israel. And that those Jews who, by the sweat of their brow, cultivated the soil, acquired a moral right to it.

"Israelis in the early days abhorred the use of outside labor," Reuven continues. "We believed that a Jewish working class—at the beginning in the fields and later in the factories—was essential to the healthy growth of the Jewish state. In short, we believed we must do the hard labor ourselves. Now, however, the young people have a different philosophy. They are concerned about themselves. They say they want to find themselves and do their own thing. They shun menial, dark, 'dirty' work. As an example, the young people do not want to work in the dairy. We had so many complaints from men who did not want to clean the barns that at one time we said, well, let's shut the dairy down. But then it was pointed out we couldn't shut it down because this was one part of the moshav that was making money.

"To keep the dairy farm going, we had to hire Arab labor. Ours is no different from other farms throughout Israel. Jews all over Israel hire Arab labor. Many Israelis call our reliance on Arab workers on our farms 'a cancer in our body.' We are locked into an undesirable state of dependence. On some farms, agricultural labor at harvest time can often be one hundred percent Arab."

One Friday evening I ask Aviva if she will go to the synagogue with me. She agrees, and getting two kerchiefs for our heads we start the short walk to the small moshav synagogue.

"This will be the first time since 1973 that I have gone to the synagogue. In that year I went to pray for victory in the war. However, Reuven and I are not religious. In this respect, we are typical of most Israelis who live in a state based on Orthodox Judaism although they do not practice nor believe in its tenets. I accept Judaism for its traditions," Aviva says.

Most Israelis are perhaps like most Americans who live in what is termed a Christian nation, but who are not necessarily religious nor necessarily believe in Christ. There is a big difference, however; the United States has separation of church and state, whereas Israel does not.

"We built our synagogue primarily for the parents of those who

work at the *moshav*. But the community as a whole is not religious,"
Aviva explains. "We have only one Orthodox person living here. He
is the only one who won't work on the Sabbath. But the *moshav*
work goes on everyday. For instance, the cows also have to be milked
on Saturdays. So you can't have someone sitting back. But his job is
not important so we can do without him on the Sabbath. He is trying
to bring his children up as Orthodox Jews, but he has no support
from us. And the children do not want it.

"Reuven and I cannot say, We know there is a God. But we keep
the Jewish traditions. We have come from somewhere. So we light
the candles on the Sabbath, and we keep all the festivals. And on
certain festivals I send the children to the synagogue."

Inside the synagogue I note it seats about fifty persons. I see perhaps twenty-five men and a few young children, mostly boys, up
front, with their fathers. Aviva and I join a half-dozen women in the
last pew. We sit alongside a woman whose husband is chosen by the
cantor to display the Torah, and we and the other women curiously
watch not the husband so much as his wife, whose face reflects pride
in his recognition. Traditionally, she lives vicariously in his role; she
gains her prestige not from herself as an individual but from being
attached to a man who is recognized. "The honor to display the
Torah is bestowed regularly on first one man, then another, but
never on a woman," Aviva tells me in a whisper. Still, the women
are progressing. At least in this synagogue Aviva and I and the other
women were permitted to sit in the same hall with the men.

Aviva and I, standing and reading from the Scripture, share a
prayer book with Hebrew on one page and English on the other. As
she speaks in Hebrew, I read the translation. "Thou hast chosen us
from all peoples . . ."

Such Scripture has instilled in many fundamentalist Jews as well
as fundamentalist Christians the belief that a God created billions of
people and chose the Jews as his favorite.

On our walk back home, we discuss this fundamentalist
interpretation.

"The idea of thinking yourself better than everybody else is pure
arrogance," Aviva says. "People say God and God and God. Some
people think God is an old man with a big beard sitting up in the
sky. I don't know what God is. Perhaps God is love.

"I just try to be good. Yet I feel everybody has to have a belief in something. My belief is in trying to lead a good life, trying not to hurt other people, and trying to get the best out of life.

"Sometimes you need something to explain why things happened, so you say God. God isn't just Mother Nature. The main thing is, you try to be at peace with other people, and you don't deliberately harm people. That's good enough.

"This is the country I'm living in because I was born in a Jewish family. I was born in England. My father was born in England. My grandparents were born in Russia. But the roots of Judaism come from Israel." Yet Aviva insists it is not the religion of Judaism that made her Jewish.

"Most people when they think of a Jew think of the religion. They don't accept being Jewish as a nationality. Why? Because all these thousands of years we didn't have a homeland. Just because a Christian does not go to church every Sunday doesn't mean he's not a Christian. But a lot of people think that if a Jew does not go to a synagogue and does not believe in God, then he is not a Jew.

"Being Jewish has nothing to do with being religious. For me, anyway. It is my nationality. That I didn't have a homeland wasn't my fault. I am here now. I've come back to it. It's my homeland. It is written in the Bible that this is the land of the Jews, the Promised Land for the chosen people."

After making a case for her Jewishness as a national feeling, Aviva returns to religion. "Through religion, that's how we've managed to stay together. So many other races have disappeared from the face of the earth. Look at all the terrible things that have happened, yet we are still here. There has to be a reason for it.

"That is why I sometimes think it's wrong that we are going away from our religion and trying to be like other people. It is a way of being wiped off the face of the earth." Aviva adds that while she came to Israel in search of her heritage she also realizes that it is "all over the world." Traditions, customs, celebrations—all have been handed down.

"For instance, many of our festivals have roots in the same pagan rites. The festivals of the different religions always come about the same time of the year, and many of them are observed with the same ritual. Christians have Christmas and light up a Christmas tree and have a big meal. Just before Christmas, Jews have the holiday Hanukkah, the Festival of Lights. Back in pagan times, also, they had a festival of the lights at this time of the year because it was winter and there was no electricity so people made their light earlier. These things have been handed down. All the peoples we know have fed on traditions of others, have borrowed from older legends and myths."

One evening, Aviva and another *moshav* resident, Marsha, a young woman from Newark, New Jersey, are discussing what Judaism means in their lives. Aviva again says that it is not her religion but her nationality.

"The Jews who escaped persecution in Europe and came to settle in Israel were Ashkenazic Jews," Marsha comments. "And I held the belief, until settling in Israel, that the country was populated entirely by European or Anglo-Saxon Jews. I was surprised when I came here to learn that the Oriental Jews are the majority. And these Oriental Jews have far more ancient strains than the Ashkenazic Jews."

"Aren't we all a Semitic people?" Aviva asks.

"I do not believe the Jews are a race," Marsha replies. "There are fixed categories of race—Negroid, Caucasian, Mongoloid. Both the Oriental Jews and the Arabs are Semitic people. But I can't see a blond, blue-eyed Polish or American Jew and think of him or her as of the Semitic race. I do not believe we Anglo-Saxons of Jewish faith originally came from Palestine. There was never a pure German race, and in my mind there is no pure Jewish race. I believe myself to be a mixture of many races. In the course of history men and women of different faiths intermarried, and many who married Jews converted to Judaism."

Later, as Aviva and I wash dishes, she refers to our going to the synagogue together, and she asks if I had felt an outsider.

No, I reply. I had not thought of it. I was among Western people who looked, dressed, and held thought patterns similar to mine. In the varied synagogues I had attended I saw more differences between Jew and Jew, say between an old Yemenite and Aviva, than in other instances I had found between Jew and Muslim or Jew and Christian.

Aviva and I felt and thought very much alike. She said maybe God was love. No one to my mind in any sect has come up with a better definition.

In the West Bank

Until going to the Arab-inhabited West Bank, I was like millions of others who read headlines about it but did not know what or where it is. I did not know the size of the West Bank and exactly who are the people living there and why most world leaders say the West Bank is the key to peace between Jews and Arabs.

One young Palestinian woman named Nahla answers the questions this way. "The West Bank," she said, "along with the Gaza Strip, is all we have left of our Palestine."

Israel conquered territories, including Arab East Jerusalem, the West Bank, and the Gaza Strip, in the war of 1967. When the fighting stopped, an Israeli military government took over the political and legal authority of Egypt in the Gaza Strip and of Jordan in East Jerusalem and the West Bank.

The West Bank and Gaza differ in history and in the magnitude of their problems, but they are similar in that both are inhabited by Palestinian Arabs who are under Israeli military occupation and who want to be free of it. In speaking of Israeli-occupied territories in this book, I deal only with the lands inhabited by Palestinian Arabs, and for this reason I do not include the Golan Heights, a part of Syria now militarily occupied by Israel.

The visitor to the West Bank and the Gaza Strip has one overwhelming impression: each area is postage-stamp small. The Gaza Strip is a one-hundred square mile strip of land that faces the Mediterranean Sea. It touches Egypt and Israel, but not the West Bank.

The West Bank lies west of the Jordan River—and of course west of Jordan itself. It is an area of only 2,165 square miles, only slightly larger than the state of Delaware, which has 2,057 square miles. The West Bank, shaped somewhat like a kidney, extends only eighty miles from north to south. Its east-west boundaries lie up to thirty-four miles from the Jordan River and as little as nine miles from the Mediterranean Sea.

Topographically, the West Bank has two distinct areas. The terrain rises westward across a broad ridge of hills and mountains that runs down the far slopes toward the Mediterranean Sea. The highlands extend from the Hebron area in the south to Jenin in the north, passing through Bethlehem, Jerusalem, Ramallah and Nablus.

The Jordan Valley, the second distinct area, extends from the Dead Sea—690 feet below sea level—and Jericho, one of the most ancient of cities, in the south, to the borders with Beisan, Israel, in the north.

Nearly a million Palestinian Arabs live in the West Bank and Gaza.

Once I drove from Israel with Aviva and Reuven Neuman and other residents of *Moshav* Timoren for an all-day outing and picnic in the West Bank. Many of the Israelis were traveling into the Arab-inhabited West Bank for the first time.

Aviva, who is an especially sensitive woman, did not feel comfortable picnicking on the West Bank. Our chartered bus filled with about forty Israelis pulled into an area that I later learned had been an Arab town, one demolished by Jewish terrorists fighting to establish Israel in 1948.

As we spread our blankets and basket lunches, Aviva asks her Israeli companion, "Doesn't this land belong to some Arab?"

"No," one young Israeli answers, "It belongs to us."

From our grassy knoll, I look out over ancient terraced lands of Arab farms. In the distance, I see the exclusively Arab town of Ramallah, as well as the small Palestinian university called Bir Zeit. It would be unthinkable, I knew, for any group of Palestinians to leave the West Bank and go onto lands inhabited by Israelis and spread their blankets and open their baskets and enjoy a picnic. But then there is a difference. As the young Israeli told Aviva, the West Bank "belongs to us." The Israelis say that. But no international court or world government, including the United States, agrees that Israel owns the West Bank.

After lunch Aviva and I climb an embankment and look across to Israel. It is a clear day and we can easily see Tel Aviv and the Mediterranean. "You see how close Tel Aviv is to the Arabs," Aviva remarks, adding "It is our proximity to the West Bank and the Palestinian Arabs that worries many Israelis. And for this reason many Israelis want to annex the West Bank." Reflecting on this, she adds, "We want security. Yet we know that extending our borders will not assure us peace. We can extend them in any direction and we will have Arabs as neighbors. So we must learn to live with Arabs."

"The Arabs, in general, are not the people who bother us," one elderly man reminds the group, "The Arabs can only threaten us by what they can do. It is the *Palestinian* Arabs who gnaw at our hearts. They threaten us with what they are, rival claimants to this land. They were here for thousands of years before any of us arrived. And they are over there in Ramallah and all around. And they keep saying, 'It is our land.'"

Later, in Tel Aviv, I attended a "Peace Now" rally, attended by eighty thousand Israelis who want to live in peace with their Palestinian neighbors. Meanwhile, however, a small, fanatical, right-wing, ultra-conservative group of Israelis, many of them recent immigrants from America, who have banded together into what they call the Bloc of the Faithful, Gush Emunim, and are fully armed, say they will start a war if necessary to gain a Greater Israel, one that would include all that is left of historic Palestine and, as a Gush follower told me, the present nations of Lebanon and Jordan as well.

In several of the Jewish colonies, all illegal under international law, I saw that native-born Americans comprise one-third to one-half the settlers. Many of the Gush settlers regard the American-born Rabbi Meir Kahane, founder of the United States-based Jewish Defense League, as their hero. Once in Ramallah, I watched Kahane and his followers arrive in the central square and begin shouting to native Palestinians, "Get out of this country! This is our country!" At night, in Ramallah and Nablus and other Arab West Bank towns, Kahane and Gush settlers have roamed the streets, shooting wildly, smashing windows, and terrorizing the Palestinian civilians.

Gush Emunim settlers who are encamped not far from the Palestinian University of Bir Zeit have on several occasions raided the campus. One day when I am at Bir Zeit I decide to go to Newi Tzuf to visit the armed Jewish colonists who so terrorize students as well as the other West Bank Palestinians. I bargain with a Palestinian taxi driver who, for six dollars, agrees to drive me to the Jewish colony.

Leaving Bir Zeit, we soon are in a kind of wilderness, inhabited, it seems, only by me and this driver, dark-skinned and silent. I realize this Arab could easily do with me what he willed, rob me or rape me. I decide on a friendly approach.

Has he lived here long? I ask.

Yes, he replies, he was born here as was his father and his father's father. As he talks, I look out to an ancient land, with groves of olives that have been tended by a peasant people for thousands of years. The Palestinian Arabs lived through four hundred years of the Ottoman Empire, and they lived through the English occupation, and they lived through Jordanian rule—and they always grew their olives and tended their sheep on the plots handed down from father to son. Some have documents of title, as we in the United States have papers to prove ownership of land, but many Palestinian peasants, having lived under so many various overlords, do not have papers to prove that the land worked by their father's father's father is rightfully theirs.

There are three categories of land in the West Bank. First, there is private, or so-called Mulk land, for which the Arab owner has clear title. Second, there is land for which there is no clear title but which the Arab farmers have cultivated for generations and which is registered with Jordan's Ministry of Finance for tax purposes. Third, there is land that also has been cultivated for generations and that, before the British mandate, was under the title of the Ottoman Sultan. Farmers claim that their ownership of this land was recognized by the British and Jordanian governments.

The third category, termed Miri land under the Ottoman law, constitutes about 70 percent of the West Bank, and it is the land on which most of the Palestinian farmers have lived for thousands of years. They make no distinction in their minds between Miri and Mulk. In both cases, the facts, as the Palestinians see those facts, are the same. It is Palestinian Arab land, and they repeat endlessly: we and our forebears have lived on this land as long as memory serves. Within Israel proper, the Israeli courts have abolished the distinction between deed-in-hand, so-called Mulk land, and Miri land. All Miri land, regardless of whether or not it is being farmed, is considered private property to which the state has no claim. However, the Israelis say that the Miri land on the West Bank is not private property but is state land and, because they designate it state land, they have the right to take it.

Along the way, the Palestinian driver tells me something of the Jewish settlement I will visit. "It is near an Arab village called Nebi Salah. During the time of the Ottoman Empire, the Turks built an old fortress there. When the British came in, they used the fortress as a district police station; when they left, it was abandoned. Then, in 1977, a few Jews moved in and occupied the old fortress. They sat there, claiming the land. Later they built a big fence and enclosed fifty acres of land belonging to the villagers of Nebi Salah. The farmers were cultivating grain and orchards there, but the Jews told the farmers they would shoot them if they attempted to go and tend their fields."

The landowners, he continues, got an attorney who filed a request before the Supreme Court of Israel, asking to show cause why the Jews should not evacuate the lands of the Nebi Salah villagers. "Apparently the lawsuit got stuck there," the driver concludes.

In the distance I see the old fortress, a large prisonlike building, with the Israeli blue-and-white flag flying overhead. The Palestinian driver stops. I get out of the taxi and walk to a soldier's sentry house, and a stern-faced soldier, rifle at the ready, approaches me. I see meanness, hatred. But this is in my own eyes. Fashioned by my own fears. I am seeing his gun—a gun I hate because it kills. I quickly dismiss this thought. I know behind his gun and behind his uniform is a man like thousands of men I have known in Vietnam and Korea, Germany, Russia, and China, a man who is performing a duty he is ordered to do. Tens of thousands of Israelis oppose their government's West Bank settlements and many have demonstrated against the necessity of serving their Army duty at these illegal encampments in the Arab-inhabited West Bank.

Where is he from? I ask the Israeli guard. "Austria," he replies. We talk about the Danube, and when I leave, to continue walking, I have forgotten the gun and I am aware of a lonely man. But again a gun comes to mind. I recall that a settler from this encampment drove onto Bir Zeit campus, shooting wildly and seriously injuring one student and I know that this same settler continues to reside here and he could have that same gun aimed at me.

Inside the fenced area, I walk near the old fortress, and to one side of it, among a cluster of prefabricated houses, I see a woman. I approach her and introduce myself. She tells me she is Malka Nisan, a native-born American, and she invites me inside her home for coffee and cake. Blond and blue-eyed, she says she "immediately identified" with the Jewish people of Israel. But within a few minutes she spells out her loneliness and frustration. "It is not easy," she tells me in an off-guard moment, adjusting to "a different language, a different culture."

The "different language" is Hebrew, one that was not generally spoken for two thousand years and became a modern language only in this century, after the creation of the state of Israel. And the "different culture" to which she must adjust—if she lives in the West Bank—is Arab culture, a culture that is native to Oriental Jews and, of course, to Arabs.

If she has problems adjusting to a "different" language and a "different" culture, with whom or with what had she so easily identified? Since she seldom leaves the old fortress, she can only meet and talk with other light-skinned immigrants like herself. And they "easily identify" with each other because they are bound by a territorial-political ideology.

I spend most of the day with this lonely woman and others like her, who while away their time tending children and awaiting the return of their husbands, who work in Tel Aviv. She herself never leaves the compound unless accompanied by several men armed with an arsenal of weapons.

"We have our own bus that goes between here and Tel Aviv," she explains, adding that I will be able to use it when I leave. I reply that since I do not wish to go to Tel Aviv but rather to Ramallah and back to Jerusalem, I will go to the highway and flag a passing car. Her mouth drops in surprise.

"There are only Arabs out there! They will kill you!"

Has she ever met a Palestinian or talked with a Palestinian? I ask.

"They are all terrorists!" she replies. She identifies with me, feeling we are two of a kind, having the same cultural background. It is us—and "them," the enemy. She is solicitous, sisterly.

Insisting the Palestinians will not murder me, I bid her goodbye. She accompanies me to the sentry gate and watches as I walk to the highway and after a wait of ten minutes hail a car. It is driven by a dark-faced Arab male who has a dark-faced Arab male companion. I climb in, somewhat shaken because I have been influenced by Malka's fears. The two Palestinians, en route to Bir Zeit, leave me there, where I get a shared-taxi into Jerusalem.

In Arab East Jerusalem I talk with the American Consul, Donald Kruse, relating that I found several American professors at the Palestinian Bir Zeit University and, on the other side, I had found many native Americans among the fanatical Gush settlers, and I remind him: all hold American passports. He talked of the danger, saying, "The day an American-born Gush settler raids Bir Zeit and shoots an American professor or an American student there, I'm in real trouble. Both sides will come running to me, holding their passports, and shouting, 'I'm an American! Protect me, help me.'"

Some days later I ride in a shared, seven-passenger Arab taxi south from Jerusalem about an hour's drive to Hebron, one of the West Bank cities with the least Western influence. A visitor does not look here for McDonald's, Holiday Inn, Greyhound, or American Express. For a moment I feel lost in a multitude of strangers who do not share my culture, thought patterns, values, or language. I move among Arab women and men in long, flowing attire, the Arab merchants wearing the traditional Arab headgear called a keffiya. I feel myself swept in a vortex of sensuous spices, strong Arabic coffee, ripened fruit. I hear voices that speak only Arabic. I see signs only in Arabic. I feel in a virtual sea that moves to a rhythm that is Arabic.

Hebron, like Nablus, is a heart-center of Palestinian sentiment. Into this all-Arab setting, Israeli settlers moved—building skyscraper housing complexes that rise imposingly over ancient, low-lying Arab homes and look like Miami Beach moved to the Casbah. The settlement is called Kiryat Arba.

In Hebron, I come to know an Arab photographer, Abu Ghannam, who makes his living taking pictures of weddings and developing and selling film, and I meet a dozen or so members of his extended family. "Try to imagine how they treat us!" he tells me once when he and I are walking in downtown Hebron. At this moment, we see approaching us two white-skinned, blue-eyed Israeli civilians, armed with clubs and guns, and holding German Shepherd patrol dogs on leashes.

"They take the law unto themselves," Abu Ghannam says. "The Israeli government is responsible. The government urges them to take our land, to make their settlements. And the government gives them all the weapons they want."

Do these vigilantes, I ask, often walk the streets with guns, clubs and dogs?

"They do as they please. One night my family and I were seated at home, watching TV, and they burst into our living room, demanding that we pack our belongings and leave Hebron. They were shouting, 'This is not a land for Arabs.'" Abu Ghannam later showed me his car. "Look. When they were leaving they smashed my windshield. They have done that to dozens of cars of Palestinians living in Hebron."

One day a young Jewish immigrant from Denmark, a follower of the extremist Rabbi Moshe Levinger, one of the founders of Gush Emunim, walked into the center of Hebron. No witness has yet been identified who saw what happened. But suddenly the Arab merchants closed their stands and disappeared. Later the Jewish immigrant was found dead.

Following the murder, the Israeli army clamped a discriminatory ten-day curfew on the center of Hebron. The Israeli Army confined Arab residents to their homes while permitting Jewish settlers, armed with rifles and pistols, to stroll through the streets.

"They entered the home of two Arab stonecutters, Abdel Idris and his brother Hussein," Ghannam reports. "They beat their children, as well as Abdel's pregnant wife. I know Abdel, and he told me the Jews kept shouting, 'If you won't leave your home, we will kill you.'"

Then the Arabs took revenge. They shot six Jewish settlers, among them Eli Hazeev, a recent immigrant from America. He was born James Mahon, Jr. He had fought in Vietnam and in motorcycle gang wars. Then he went to Israel and converted to Judaism in order, as he told friends, "to fight." His acquaintances in Hebron said, "He wanted to die fighting." His parents, from Alexandria, Virginia, stood at his grave. They said they were sorry he died, "but we deplored his violence."

From Hebron, I travel to Nablus to visit a controversial settlement called Elon Moreh. Prime Minister Begin had gone to the dedication of this settlement and promised the dozen or so Jewish squatters sitting on Palestinian farmland, "There will be many more Elon Morehs."

In Nablus, I ask a Palestinian taxi driver if he will take me to Elon Moreh. He is reluctant. "They are fanatics. And they are all armed." Nevertheless, he agrees to take me there. Once I am inside the colony, I move among the prefabricated houses and find the wife of an Israeli, whose husband continues to live in Tel Aviv. She invites me to stay with her. Then I begin to take meals with other settlers, about half of them native-born Americans.

One evening—it happened to be New Year's but no one was celebrating—I sit in the prefabricated home of two of the Jewish settlers, Zev and Rochelle Saffer. Saffer is a native of Monsey, New Jersey, who worked for the American Cyanamid Company before moving to the West Bank. He is about thirty, a man of uncommon good looks, with blond hair and blue eyes and a voice that even when he is emotional remains soft and well modulated.

"Growing up, I felt myself an American—a Jewish American," Saffer relates. "Then I became active in a college Zionist youth movement. I felt a stronger identity as a Jew. I felt a minority. Yet, I had non-Jewish friends whose grandparents had not been born in America, whereas I was a third-generation American.

"I reached a decision that I wasn't in my own land. I did not feel America was my country. As I started to vote, I would ask: Is this candidate good for the Jews? Is this candidate good for Israel?

"I said to myself, I want to be in a land where I feel it is my land and my country. Where I would never be considered someone who does not belong."

His statement implies that people in his hometown in New Jersey considered him "someone who does not belong." But earlier he said he had suffered no discrimination there. And his idea that he had now chosen a place where he was welcomed, where everyone would recognize he belonged, was hardly in touch with reality.

"So we came here," Saffer concludes, "because we want to give the maximum service to our homeland."

It is difficult if not impossible for me to think that blond-haired, blue-eyed, fair-skinned Saffer—and the other recently arrived American natives—ever had roots they could trace to this land of dark-skinned Semitic people. We know that men and women have always traveled the world and intermarried. And that because of wars, love, or conviction, men and women have been converted to first one religion, then another. As modern examples, Sammy Davis, Jr. and Elizabeth Taylor both are Jews because they converted to Judaism.

Terms such as Hebrew, Israelite, Judean, Judaism, and the Jewish people are used synonymously to suggest a historic continuity, whereas they were in fact different people at different times in history with varying ways of life, who continually intermarried with Amorites, Canaanites, Phoenicians, and other Semitic ancestors of the present-day Arabs.

Most of the white-skinned immigrants such as Saffer may be descendants of converts to Judaism. Studies seem to indicate that the overwhelming majority of today's Jews are descendants of the eighth-century converts to Judaism, the Khazars, who settled in what is now Southern Russia between the Volga and the Don, and adopted Judaism seven centuries after the destruction of Jerusalem in A.D. 70.

Saffer owns grocery stores in various West Bank Jewish settlements, and hired Paul Fuchs from Hillside, New Jersey, to run his store in Elon Moreh. "I am overqualified for the job," Fuchs, who has a Ph.D. in chemistry, jokes. He seems, however, representative of the settlers: highly educated, they yet desire a dogma, a certitude. In this respect they are no different from fundamentalists of the Christian and Muslim sects.

"I have not 'found myself' in Israel," Fuchs admits, and he talks about the difficulties of emigrating from America.

"One-third of those who come here return home. You get hit by a stone block of bureaucracy. Salaries are one-third or one-half of what they are in the States. Yet the prices here are the equivalent of or higher than those in the States. Appliances, for instance, are sky high. I could put up with all this, but"—and Fuchs gives me a sad look—"the worst thing is, you face discrimination here. The Jews who were born here resent the new immigrants."

Linda and Bobby

I have written of visiting Jewish settlements in the south, near Hebron, and in the north, near Nablus, but actually the first settlement I visited was near Bethlehem, and here I came to know Linda and Bobby. It happened in a rather circuitous way. After hearing of a West Jerusalem Jewish agency that conducts bus tours to the Gush Emunim settlements, I go to an office on King George Street near the Plaza Hotel, and I find myself seated across a desk from a pleasant young man, David Ben-Naeh. I tell him that rather than take a conducted tour, I want to live awhile in one of the settlements. He dials a few numbers, then hands me the phone and I talk to a settler who tells me his name is Bobby Brown, and who says fine, I can stay in their home. We agree on a time and place to meet later that week, in Jerusalem.

At the appointed time I am sitting in a small reception room of the Church of Scotland Guest House. Guests sip tea and listen to a pianist playing Bach. Suddenly the music stops, and all eyes rivet on a moving figure who carries a submachine gun. Each face registers a fear that we are under attack. In this stunned moment of silence, I approach the man, certain he is my host, and walk from the Guest House with Bobby Brown.

Brown, about thirty, is of average height, soft-spoken, and outfitted in sturdy Western clothes preferred by men who win frontiers. He seems very American, in that he walks with that gait of assurance we associate with the world's greatest power, and he makes a new acquaintance easily; both of us are quickly on a first-name basis. It is apparent that Bobby Brown from the Bronx thinks his name precisely fits his personality, because he has not bothered to change to a Hebrew name, as many immigrants do.

"I have not given up America, only added Israel," Bobby tells me. Bobby and I drive south from Jerusalem and within minutes are

46

on the West Bank of the Jordan, the territory that, except for armed Jewish soldiers and armed Jewish civilians such as Brown, is occupied exclusively by Palestinian Arabs. We pass Shepherds' Field and Bethlehem. Along the way, Bobby Brown explains that he left a high-paying job in New York to come to this ancient land and take up arms with a militant Zionist movement.

"Gush Emunim is not a movement where you go into an office, sign up, get a membership card, and pay dues," Brown explains. "We do have an office, but we don't have any membership cards. Still it is a growing movement. And we are dedicated to one goal: to drive the Arabs out and create a Greater Israel."

More nationalistic than most Israeli natives, Brown sees himself and Linda as no different from the Jews who in the 1920s and 1930s settled in the choice coastal sections of Palestine and began the struggle that ended in the establishment of Israel in 1948. To Bobby's mind, however, that was only the first phase of the struggle.

He wants not only the territories the United Nations "recommended" the Jews be given in 1947 and the territories the Israelis conquered militarily, he wants all of historic Palestine, as well as other Arab lands. He mentions an Israel that extends to the Euphrates and includes Jordan.

"We do not see lines on a map," Bobby says. "The border will be made after we settle the area. In every place where we make a settlement we will never abandon that settlement. We know all of Israel's towns and villages have been founded on what once were Arab towns and villages. We want all the Arabs to leave, and if coming to settle here means we must be in a continual state of warfare with the Arabs, then so be it. If we can't have a Greater Israel, then we don't want peace."

Jews planted their first colony on the West Bank soon after the 1967 war. "A group of Jewish settlers moved into a former army camp, fenced off a parcel of land and called their new home Kafr Etzion," Brown relates.

It is a matter of record that the Jews, in taking the land, forced Palestinian farmers from it. The Palestinians complained to authorities that the Jewish settlers "stole sixty-five acres of land we have farmed for generations." I mention this Palestinian Arab claim to Bobby.

"What can they do? Possession is nine-tenths of the law," Brown
replies, adding that classical Zionist strategy involves "establishing
facts." Also, in "establishing facts," Bobby says, "we must be clever
and use deliberate ambiguity, concealing ultimate objectives." International law (Article 49 of the Geneva Convention) bars an occupying power, in this case Israel, from settling civilians in occupied
territory, in this case the West Bank.

"But security outposts are permitted. So, you say you need the
land for security, to establish an army camp. By saying it's for the
army, you eliminate the need to file formal expropriation orders.
Then, once you get the land, you move civilians in." Bobby pauses,
obviously pleased by such Gush Emunim political chicanery, which
might be applauded in some circles as statecraft but by whatever
name cannot be reconciled with religion.

In the case of Tekoa, the Israelis confiscated the land from Palestinian farmers and then moved in Russian Jewish immigrants. But
the Russians hated Tekoa and left for America, an option that a big
majority of the Russian Jews permitted to leave the Soviet Union
have taken. As for Tekoa, "the place was folding until we moved in,"
Bobby says of himself and the other native Americans.

Bobby and I continue driving through the Judean hills past an
Arab village called Rifida. "You can see how empty all this land is.
It is nothing but rock and sand—really useless," Bobby insists.

As twilight turns to darkness Brown and I turn a corner and I see
a fenced-off enclosure illuminated with high-powered searchlights
like an enormous football field—lights that on this ancient landscape
jar one's sense of time and place. The searchlights and the security
guardhouses make the fenced-off area look like an army compound
or a prison.

Brown flips off his headlights, "so they will know we are not the
enemy," and pulls up to the security guardhouse, where a uniformed,
armed Israeli soldier who sees Brown every day, nevertheless asks for
a password. Brown gives it. We drive inside, park alongside a half-
dozen cars, and we get out, carrying with us sacks of groceries Brown
has purchased in Jerusalem.

Since the 1967 war, Israel has built one hundred settlements in
the Arab-inhabited Gaza and the West Bank. About twelve thousand Jews live in these settlements, which range in size from the five-

hundred-fifty-family urban development at Kiryat Arba, near Hebron, to this outpost at Tekoa that appears little more than a façade to establish a Jewish presence in an otherwise all-Arab area. Bobby frankly admits the purpose: "to make it impossible for the Palestinians to unite and operate a continuous territorial entity. They will be cut off by our settlements. Then they will have little choice but to leave."

That evening, Linda, twenty-eight, tall, dark-haired, and sharp of mind, holds one-year-old Geula as we sit informally around a card table eating supper. Linda gladly tells me the route that brought her to this lonely, desolate settlement.

"I was born in 1952 in Yonkers, New York, and I grew up there. I am a third-generation American. My parents seldom went to the synagogue. As a small child, I remember my father sometimes went, and then he stopped going. And my mother never went. They were in the mainstream—assimilated as Americans. For example, they did not object when my brother married a Gentile." The marriage did not bother Linda at the time but now she objects to such marriages. She and Bobby agree with the religious laws in Israel that stipulate a Jew can marry only another Jew, that is, a person with a Jewish mother, or a person who is converted by an orthodox rabbi. In Israel, all marriages must remain in the hands of the orthodox clergy.

Until she was well into her teens Linda, like her parents, did not go to the synagogue and also felt herself assimilated. "And then college changed my life. I joined the first Zionist club formed at the State University of New York at Stonybrook, Long Island. But I never told my parents about the club and its great influence on me. I saw no reason in getting them aggravated."

Eventually, however, she told her parents because the Zionists gave her a ticket to visit Israel. It was in Israel that she met Bobby, who also was sent there by a Zionist club—one formed at Long Island University, Brooklyn College campus.

"We returned to New York and continued to attend Zionist youth meetings. Then after we got married," Linda relates, "we shocked my parents by saying we were moving to Israel. My parents thought that all of this was to be blamed on Bobby. And I just told them at that point that, No, it was my own decision from years ago.

"I determined to marry an orthodox Jew and keep a kosher

kitchen," Linda continues as she dips a spoon into first one, then a second oversized jar to extract peanut butter and jelly, ingredients for the sandwiches we are making for ourselves. Linda, in talking of keeping a kosher kitchen and abiding by ancient dietary laws that permit eating meat only from an animal that has cloven hooves and chews its cud, wants to imagine herself living the type of life that a great-great grandmother back in Poland might have lived. In reality she was far removed from it, operating with a large Frigidaire and an electrical can-opener, and frozen orange juice. Yet, even when serving peanut butter and jelly sandwiches, she could boast that she was kosher.

One evening a group of the fair-skinned American settlers and I sit under the stars. The men and women talk about why they left loved ones and friends to come to a wilderness and live in prefab houses and settle a land that has been occupied by dark-skinned Oriental people for as long as there are written records.

"There are pluses and minuses to living here," Elie Birnbaum, a psychologist from New York begins. Others in our circle include Elie Birnbaum's wife Leah, Linda and Bobby, and Howard and Barbara Ginsburg, from Long Island. Of the fifteen families who live in Tekoa, seven recently emigrated from the United States.

"Living here reminds me of what America was like two hundred years ago. Here you have the spirit of just starting, of being a pioneer," Birnbaum says. "I moved here right after I had undergone an operation. Some people helped me put up my bookshelves. It was like in the early days of America when people got together for house raisings. Everybody came in, everybody did something.

"I am thrilled with how democracy works at the grass roots," Birnbaum continues. "I guess if the meetings when the Constitution was adopted were like ours, the Founding Fathers must have been funny to watch. Here people yell and jump, and we all have our own ideas. You may fight for three hours about where a clothesline should be."

Tekoa is not like a kibbutz, in which property is communally owned. Each family supports itself. But these city-born immigrants now sitting on land that has been farmed for thousands of years, do not know how to farm, never having been near a tractor or a plow.

"We decided to plant flowers for export," Bobby says. "But we ran a loss."

"Oh, but the land has other values," Elie Birnbaum points out. "It is most pleasant and relaxing to come home from a hard day at the office and tend the flowers. I get home after sitting in a chair all day, and I can work in the fields and get some energy going." The overall purpose of the settlers, however, seems not to cultivate and use the land but rather to keep the Palestinians from using it.

Elie Birnbaum, Howard Ginsburg, and Bobby Brown are typical of most of the Jewish settlers on the West Bank in that they do not work the land they have taken from Palestinian farmers. Rather, they commute, about an hour's drive, to Tel Aviv or Jerusalem. Bobby works for the Jewish Agency, largely supported by funds from America, that assists immigrants to Israel. This is the official agency that sponsors such settlements as Tekoa and the other Jewish outposts in Gaza and the West Bank.

Birnbaum also commutes to Jerusalem and also works for the Jewish Agency. Ginsburg, who ran a Long Island dry-cleaning business for twenty-five years until moving to Tekoa, also commutes to Jerusalem, where he manages a food store.

"Every settler takes a financial loss by moving here," Bobby tells me, adding that he makes only a third of the salary he gained when he worked for the Metropolitan Life Insurance Company in New York.

But it is not that Brown takes a financial loss by moving to the West Bank. He took his financial loss in his initial move from New York to Israel. As other settlers had pointed out, Israeli salaries are about one-third of the salaries in the United States.

However, settlers such as Linda and Bobby have built-in economic advantages in living at Tekoa. The Israeli government encourages the West Bank settlements by providing rent-free housing to "pioneers" such as Linda and Bobby. The settlers then are able to rent their Tel Aviv or Jerusalem flats—and bank a profit of about four hundred dollars a month.

As I sit with the settlers under the stars, I see that the men keep their submachine guns on the ready.

"Guns are something people have to live with here. We will

carry arms as long as we are in a situation where there are forces that want to kill Jewish people," Bobby states. He does not say, however, that by moving into Arab land he himself is creating "forces" that want to kill Jewish people.

"All Jewish civilians living in settlements are issued licenses to carry weapons. The men have the M-15, and the women have the Uzi. If the women do not want to carry a gun, they at least keep one Uzi in the house with extra clips.

"We all go for target practice," Bobby continues. "And anytime there is a school outing, one of the parents will be armed and go along. We go through drills in case of attack. We know who is in charge of what areas, who is in charge of fire or first-aid stations, and we have a number of people trained as medics."

A sentry, David Rokeah, also armed with a submachine gun, passes on his rounds. "Sit awhile," Bobby suggests, and David, a fourth-generation Israeli, draws up a chair beside me, takes the weapon from his shoulder, and holds it close to his right side. All his life, he says, he has been "a fighter."

He joined the Israeli underground movement, called the Irgun, to fight the British when he was thirteen, and for the rest of his life he has lived with a gun at hand. "The Jews must keep fighting," he says.

The settlers all agree they must fight to take the West Bank—which they call by the old biblical name of Judea and Samaria. Ginsburg, who has been quiet until now, speaks up.

"We believe it is important for Jews to live in our own land, in Judea and Samaria." And then he adds, "We were promised all this land by God."

Barbara Ginsburg, a quiet, diminutive woman who for the past quarter of a century stayed busy managing a Long Island home and raising a family, seems a bit perplexed by the boundaries her husband says God has promised them.

"Were we promised Jordan too?" she asks, hesitantly.

By way of reply—with a long preamble, including the statement that "there is no such thing as the West Bank; it is a euphemism"—Ginsburg reassures his wife that, yes, God also promised them Jordan.

"It is filled with Bedouins and has a king," Howard explains. "All of a sudden it has become a major state in the Middle East. . . . God forbid I have to give up my land to such a country."

"The term *Palestinian* once meant Jews and Arabs alike," Bobby points out, adding that Palestine was a League of Nations mandate ruled by the British. "And when England withdrew, the Jews established Palestine as Israel." He is, of course, forgetting that in the 1947 partition the United Nations gave a portion of historic Palestine for a Jewish homeland and left the rest for the native people, the Palestinian Arabs.

"Now when people say, 'There should be a Palestinian state,' they are talking about a Palestinian Arab state," Bobby continues. "And for all intents and purposes, that already exists in Jordan. More than half the population of Jordan is Palestinian; the other half is Bedouin. So when Arabs think they should have a second state—at the expense of the Jews—we disagree."

What about the problem, I ask, of displaced Palestinian Arab farmers?

"That is an Arab problem," Brown replies. "They can go live in another Arab country, such as Jordan." Then he adjusts his gun and adds, "We did not occupy this land to one day give it back to the natives." The New York native refers to the Palestinian Arabs as "natives." But apparently he does not think these "natives" have a native land. His saying that he and others like him will never allow the Palestinian Arabs to have a homeland recalled to mind the late 1950s when I sat at an elegant dinner party in Paris, and a French banker slammed a fist on the table, exclaiming, "We French will never relinquish Algeria."

Attempting to own a people who do not want a custodian is no longer popular nor, apparently, feasible. The United States militarily occupied Japan and Germany after World War II. We placed occupying Americans there, but never sent in armed civilians to confiscate and colonize land.

"Suppose," one American said, "that at the end of World War II our government had sent civilians into West Germany or to the countryside of Japan, armed with submachine guns, and taken land that belonged to the natives. If the natives fought to defend their native land, the settlers then could call them terrorists."

Bobby has a rather last-ditch argument for confiscating Arab land on the West Bank. "If Jews cannot settle here," he says, "this will become the only place on earth from which Jews are banned."

The question of course is why does Bobby want to live on the West Bank. Does he come as a peaceful neighbor? Quite the contrary of wanting to establish peaceful relationships, the Bloc of the Faithful moves its settlers and prefabricated units by helicopters under cover of night so that Arab farmers awake one morning to find their farmland and grazing pasture confiscated and armed sentries guarding a new Jewish colony.

And Bobby indicates that by settling in the West Bank he wants to establish the right of Jews to settle any place in this world, but the Palestinians do not have the right to move onto the property that Bobby and Linda own in Jerusalem, nor, for that matter, do the Palestinians, as non-Jews, have the right to settle anywhere in the Jewish state of Israel. And Bobby will readily tell you he would be the last to grant such a right.

Bobby illustrates an example of the "special relationship" that America maintains with Israel. Bobby knows that he cannot—armed with a submachine gun—confiscate land in the Bronx or Brooklyn. And nowhere else in the world can Bobby and Linda settle by force, as they and others like them now do on the West Bank. Having a "special relationship" with Israel, sending Israel almost as much military and economic assistance as it does to all the other 99.9 percent of the world's people combined, the United States continues to pay money for the confiscation of land. Yet, such illegality would not be tolerated within the United States itself.

Once Bobby and I drove through the Judean hills, and I saw Palestinian farmers working distant fields. "You see what an empty land it is," Bobby insists, deliberately, it seems, screening out the Palestinians, and causing me to marvel at how easily he trains his eyes to see only what he desires to see. "There are thousands and thousands of uninhabited areas. Yet the media portray this area as a refugee camp with Arabs piled up on Arabs, and Jews pushing them away.

"The media report that Tekoa was built on an Arab settlement. There are no Arabs near here. Yet once we start building a permanent settlement, all of a sudden the media yell, 'Ah, you're stealing Arab land.' And Arabs say, 'Hey, this is our land.' I'm sure someone is going to come here and say, 'You forced the native population off.' Or some Jesse Jackson is going to say that this is a greater threat than Soviet troops in Cuba."

On another day I go to the Arab village of Rifida and seek out the Palestinians, who previously had farmed the land before the settlers confiscated the seven hundred fifty acres. I meet the village leader or *mukhtar*, Khahil Ahmad El-Mu'ti, a tall, slender, bearded man in his seventies, who wears a long black robe, with impressive white silk headgear.

"The Israeli authorities gave us no written notification that they would take our land. They came with their guns and they took it," the *mukhtar* says.

"We went to Bethlehem and hired a lawyer and complained. We get no help. Yet all the land is registered in the names of our people. And we have paid taxes for this land.

"Ordinarily, governments help develop the land, give loans for tractors or for wells. But the Israelis came and, rather than helping, they *took* the land from us! They threw us off the land that we had been cultivating for centuries so that they could bring someone from Russia or America to farm our land!" As we talk, outside the *mukhtar's* home, we are joined by his wife, who gives me her maiden name, Sarah Ali Said. She is a large, genial woman, dressed in the traditional Palestinian attire and surrounded by many children.

Where, I ask, was she born? "There!" and she points to the land now occupied by the prefabricated houses, an enclosed area we see in the distance. "There, where *they* are! We have always lived there. The land was owned by my grandfather's grandfather. We have for generations planted wheat and barley on that land. Each Arab family in this community had a parcel there to plant its crops. How are we going to live? We have to use the land to grow our food. Once we went to our land and planted wheat. Then when the wheat was almost ready to harvest the settlers plowed it under. And they planted beds of flowers.

"Those who come and take our land—who are they?" she continues. "They come with their blue eyes from Europe and America and say that the land belongs to them. Who can believe them? Neither they nor their blue-eyed grandfathers ever lived in this land."

Even after having their wheat plowed under, the villagers again returned and tried to farm. "But a soldier came and pointed his gun and told us, 'Any Arab who tries to plow this land will be shot.' Now no one dares to approach. When we pass by, they aim their guns at us.

"We had a well. It is inside their fence," Sarah Ali Said continues. "We can't get to it. We have to walk miles to another well. We have to pass the land that is our land. They look at us. And they laugh. The best of the land that we own, they have taken it."

Her husband adds:

"Destroying the wheat that produces bread for hungry children is not something for humans to do to other people. We tried to talk to the Jewish authorities, to explain it was our land. And the Jewish military governor told us, 'Stay away. The settlers will kill you.'"

I later talk with Dr. Paul Quiring, an American who studied West Bank land titles under sponsorship of a United States Protestant group, the Mennonites. Dr. Quiring said he verified that Palestinian farmers in the village of Rifida had indeed paid taxes "on the land which was confiscated for the settlement of Tekoa." He said the Rifida villagers lost seven hundred fifty acres of their farmland. "Now, not one person in the village is able to live off farming. The labor force is now largely employed as day laborers in Bethlehem or in Israel.

"The confiscation process is administered as if the Arab land owners have no right to the land they have bought or inherited from their fathers, have paid taxes on for years, and which has provided them with their livelihood," Dr. Quiring said.

My first visit to Tekoa was in the summer, and I return to spend a portion of the Hanukkah observation with Linda and Bobby in December. It is bitterly cold, and Linda keeps a small electrical stove running day and night. Geula has a cold. Often because of ice, snow, and high winds, Linda is trapped indoors with Geula for days on end. The couple has received more of their possessions, including high fidelity stereo equipment, a radio, and a television, from the United States. Otherwise, the household looks about the same. Again I note Linda's loneliness. Her parents had been over for a visit, and now she misses them acutely.

My impression is that Bobby loves his warrior role and that Linda is making do the best she can. As an example, Bobby once said of

Tekoa, "We immediately liked it. It looked like a place where we could have an impact, as well as start a nice, new life." But Bobby is almost never in Tekoa. It is Linda who stays home all day.

Despite being in the dangerous, controversial setting of Tekoa, Linda is nevertheless enacting the role women traditionally play—tending a child, keeping house, telling a husband goodbye, awaiting his return. One morning I watch her detain Bobby, asking plaintively if he can return somewhat earlier that evening. I do not think that Linda cares whether Bobby returns an hour or so earlier. She seems only to need to please him. Bobby, aware that I watch, reacts by clearing his throat and gives no other answer. He slings his submachine gun over his shoulder and leaves for Jerusalem.

Linda and I often work in her kitchen and talk of her life. In answer to why she has chosen to occupy by force a land owned by Arabs, she says only that she and Bobby decided to become "pioneers"—and everyone knew pioneers struggle and sacrifice. As Linda uses the word "pioneer," I see many of the accoutrements of civilization—a TV, stereo, radio, washing machine, electric stove, and, outside, an automobile. Still, there is much she does not have: a grocery store, a drugstore, a shopping center, a museum, library, theaters, operas, movies, banks. And that great convenience, when you need it, a telephone. Most of all, she admits, she misses her family and friends.

Linda confides in me that she hopes to go into Jerusalem "and get a job"—she is a qualified physical therapist—but at present she has no one with whom she can leave Geula. "And Bobby wants me to wait until she is old enough to leave in a nursery."

What about one of her neighbors? I ask. She replies that she cannot trust them with Geula.

So why has she come to that windy, lonely hill? And why has she left security for insecurity and a life of enormous controversy and stress? Geula, for example, had been born some four months prematurely, weighing only two pounds.

Before returning to Tekoa, I lived with Nahla, a sixteen-year-old Palestinian who is "trapped" in a refugee camp. Linda also is trapped, not physically but psychologically. She is trapped in a rote, a dogma, a fundamentalism. Every moment in Tekoa I feel myself two persons—one of them a sister to Linda, understanding her desire for a certitude, and the other the sister of a Palestinian who is suffering miserably because of a militant form of Zionism that leads Jews to confiscate Arab land.

One night I lay awake wondering: Why did Linda say she could not leave Geula with any of the people here? I thought the answer was, They don't trust each other. How can you trust someone who is irrational for much of the time?

They, Linda and Bobby, are dealing with other irrational people. And everybody knows you can't trust irrational people. Even when you are one of them. Except that you don't consider yourself as irrational as they are. But the fact that you know that they are irrational means that you don't leave your child with them.

Yet, Linda had said she would be glad to leave Geula with me. She said we were like sisters, and that was one of the confidences she had in me.

But then I am an outsider. She confides in me the same way a person talks to a stranger so freely for an hour or two on an airplane. Then you know you never will see that person again. You can tell a stranger many secrets.

After I returned to the United States, I visited with Dr. Aaron Cohn, a New York psychiatrist, who has been to the West Bank and made a study of the Jewish settlers there. After reading my taped interviews and manuscript, he contrasted a native-born Israeli, such as David Rokeah in Tekoa, who admitted being "a fighter" since he was thirteen, to the young New York immigrants, who must act more militantly because they have not previously experienced war.

"As 'pioneers' they have to be extra-militant. They perceive themselves in the same light as those who did a lot of the work that brought about the state. They say they are pioneers out of a learned philosophy rather than one that came about as a result of their having a practical involvement in the evolution of politics and the culture and the economy of the country.

"They perceive themselves as the pioneers they are not. And they have to exhibit a certain degree of hardness or of irrationality just to force others to see them in that same light. It is the perception of themselves as pioneers, as revolutionaries symbolized by the carrying of the guns, that makes them the saviors of the Jews in the same sense that the Ku Klux Klan or the Knights of the White

Camellia made themselves the saviors of white womanhood in the South during the Reconstruction Period.

"They have to be more verbose, more irrational, and more militant than people who are busy trying to do many of the substantial things, such as learning a profession, teaching school, educating their children, plowing fields, milking cows, or doing any of these practical chores that maybe the country could use more than they could use another militant."

I mention to the psychiatrist that many of the native-born American settlers said, as Linda said, "College changed me," adding that they became oriented to fight Israel's cause when they joined Zionist youth movements.

"In college, they are living a fairly comfortable middle-class existence with no problems. Your biggest problem is your parents, because they want to be the Jewish mother over you. And you get to college and away from home for the first time . . . and actually it becomes a revolt against the things the college stood for. And becoming Born-Again Jews and moving to the West Bank sets them apart, like the people who were in the Peace Corps in Peru, people who are willing to put up with the deprivations of a primitive or foreign culture until the aura of this New Pioneer Society wears off and they get frustrated and come back to New York, but they will still hang on to the memories.

"You are sitting there with no telephone. And it would be different if you were a more tribal or primitive person who didn't know a telephone existed, didn't know that people had operas and other comforts of life that Linda's middle-class upbringing in a New York Jewish family gave her. And then she leaves that and goes into an artificial environment, knowing that every time she wants to pick up a phone or go to a drugstore or hear an opera, she can't. That is a big contrast between what she is used to during the time she was forming her militant ideas."

He said he saw a dichotomy in someone who says she is a "pioneer," but who serves peanut butter and jelly sandwiches.

But why, I ask. The food is so typically American.

"Yes, but she's not talking about being so American; she's talking about being kosher Jewish. That's the difference. She's trying to do something that she logically is not. Psychologically, she's peanut butter and jelly. Yet she's talking about a kosher kitchen. Kosher kitchen is about as culturally oriented as you can get because there's a lot of stuff you don't do. If you are starving you wouldn't eat unclean pork; that's not a peanut-butter-and-jelly kind of existence."

They say they are religious—I interpose—but the only aspect of religion I hear is, "God gave the land to us."

"The religion has to be an underlying factor. The dogma, the fundamentalism. And the more fundamental or more conservative it is, then the more of a unifying factor, or at least they perceive it as more of a unifying factor. The religious factor has to be the only unifying factor. That's all that could bind such diverse peoples together, from Russia, South Africa, and so forth.

"They see themselves as the preservers of Jewish culture. But they can do this only in conjunction with having a visible enemy to fight, which would be the Palestinians."

Why, I ask, couldn't they have stayed in Brooklyn?

"You have it written, they can't repossess any land in Brooklyn. They have to have a cause that unites them, that holds them together in this very shaky existence. This whole idea of *pioneer*— she said she was a pioneer and everyone knew pioneers have to sacrifice and struggle—is a romantic notion that gives credence to their intrusion. You can call yourself a pioneer, and everybody knows that pioneers struggle against great odds. The credence is in enduring the deprivations of a pioneer life. And you can sustain yourself in enduring a life full of deprivation only if you have an ideology that sustains you—not a practical kind of thing but an ideology. And I don't even think that they've got that—what they have is the Palestinians to fight against."

So what Bobby says is true, I suggest, that this is just another phase of Zionism, and the Israelis believe this in their hearts. Why else would it be a unifying factor?

"You can have unifying factors other than Zionism. Zionism is still a political movement [for] political unity. It is connected, too, with the religion; that's another cementing agency, which is inseparable, really."

I don't know whether I conveyed this, I tell Dr. Cohn, but Linda seemed very lonely and she was trying to be strong.

"Sure she is; she is in an isolated place where she seldom has a legitimate excuse for leaving and she's sitting there with people she doesn't trust and probably has very little in common with. They would tell the world that all of them there are united in a single-minded cause, but that is not true. It is a superficial cultural or religious cause that is a tremendous strain and is causing a great deal of stress.

"They [the settlers] are incapable of seeing the broader picture; they see only a very narrow interest that is theirs."

The psychiatrist points out that he heard an Israeli say, "The Gush scare me." Another Israeli said, "I fear their fanaticism points ultimately to a kind of fascism or to a point where they are an authority unto themselves." But he added that most Israelis tend to accept the extreme religionists as part of the Jewish tradition that has held an often-persecuted people together for thousands of years.

"Everyone who is a 'true' Israeli can have some affinity with what the rebels are saying. And some of them are even glad that somebody is saying something in which they can believe (but are careful or fearful for some reason or other of saying). And that is a unifying feature. The support of much of that rebel element is a catalyst for unity.

"In the narrow sense you perceive them as a threat to Israeli unity, whereas in fact they are a cementing agent in Israeli politics, and that is why they are tolerated. They are serving a useful political purpose. If these settlers carrying submachine guns on the West Bank were really contrary to deep beliefs of the Israelis, they would be stopped.

"The settlements are not perceived as a total threat, or they would be stopped. So long as you can control the rebels—that is, the settlers—the situation of allowing them to take Arab land has a unifying factor or a unifying feature in the society."

I agree with all the points that Dr. Cohn makes except his last one. I think that for many years what he says has been true, but that the unifying factor is passing—or has passed. An analogy, I believe, is our war in Vietnam. For many years we felt the sacrifice and the struggle and the honor—the honor of killing Vietnamese—was worth the price, and that if we were patient we would gain victory.

Eventually, while being unified for years by the war, we were torn asunder by that war. The same, I believe, will happen with the

Israelis. Today they are being torn asunder by their "war" to gain the West Bank. But change is certain.

Returning to Jerusalem, I sat at a cafe terrace of the King David Hotel with the Jerusalem *Post* writer, Meir Merhav. He is slightly built and a chain smoker. Tears streamed down his face as he told how he and others fought in the 1940s to help establish a Jewish state, and how with force they had expelled the Arabs.

"Deeds were done that even then tore many of us apart between what we believed in and what we thought we had no choice but to do. In that bitter, bloody war, certain facts were established—boundaries, possession of land.

"Now, however, we, the colonizers, turn into colonialists," he said. "Moral corruption crept upon us stealthily. We subdued another people and, to keep them under subjugation, we have become an armed fortress.

"We constantly talk of what the Germans did to the Jews. We use the Holocaust as a political argument, to justify what we do to the Arabs. We constantly equate the horrors then and there with the dangers here and now."

Merhav points out that a defense posture includes more than tanks, planes, and missiles. It must include "economic viability and social integrity." He does not believe the settlements serve either. "There is the invocation of exaggerated and often false security arguments, while the true aim lurking behind them is annexation based on Messianic myth." He adds that for the first time in the history of his country, reservists are reluctant to spend thirty days a year guarding the settlements.

The settlers, he continues, "moved by a fanatic religionism and deluding themselves that Bible quotations can be a basis for claims in international practice and law, misperceive the balance of real forces in the world and ride roughshod over all moral standards except those they invoke as divine revelation."

Moreover, the settlements, he argues, would actually hamper the smooth conduct of war and the country's ability to deal cohesively with a frontal attack. In the event of war, a large Israeli military force would be required to protect the Jewish colonies now planted in the midst of Arab populations. And they would deter, not aid, the military operations.

"The Gush Emunim dogma, the holy egotism, that condones the grabbing of Arab land in the name of old Scripture, converts Israel's friends around the world into her enemies, and serves only destructive purposes," Merhav concludes.

JUDAISM
CHRISTIANITY
ISLAM

With Christians in Jerusalem: The Old Walled City

In the prologue, I mentioned that I would write about a young Arab Christian woman named Mervat, who poses the question, Will Christians continue to leave the land of Christ? Before I write about Mervat, who lives on the outskirts of Bethlehem, let me first introduce some of the Christians I met within the Old Walled City of Jerusalem.

The overwhelming majority of Christians in the Holy Land are Arab Christians, such as Mervat and her family. But of course there are exceptions, such as Michael, an Armenian Christian tour guide who has dubbed himself "Walking Michael." I join a group in a walking tour of the Old City of Jerusalem with "Walking Michael," and we pass the Armenian quarters. Michael explains that Armenia was a former kingdom of Southwest Asia, south of the Caucasus Mountains, now divided among Russia and Turkey and Iran.

"We Armenians are the oldest Christian community within the Walled City," he relates. Then, philosophically, he continues, "We can't help how we are born. For instance, I have an Ethiopian friend who lives in Jerusalem. He wants to stay here. He has black skin. We are products of our parents and our environment. I have parents who are Armenians. I am not Arab. I am not Jew. So what am I?"

"You are an Israeli," an American in our group suggests.

"No, I am not Israeli," Michael replies. "I am Christian."

Some weeks pass and I encounter Michael in the Via Dolorosa. He volunteers that it's his birthday, so I invite him for a drink and we walk to Cafe Citadel near Jaffa Gate.

"I have so few opportunities living under the Israeli occupation. I would leave Jerusalem if I were not so old," he laments.

And how old is he?

"Thirty-nine," he replies in a tired voice.

The Christians who are leaving are for the most part young, those like Banayout Younan, nineteen. "For as long as my forebears can remember, we have been Christians living in the Old City," Younan says. His father, works as a tailor, as did his father and his father's father. Younan is tall and robust, with a light complexion, dark eyes, and an open face that indicates he never meets a stranger. He moves with the head-on, confident stride of a Western salesman.

Once he invites me to visit his home in the Old City. We leave a well-traveled corrider, climb steps, and enter the living quarters of Banayout's family. He introduces me to his mother, a Greek Orthodox Christian, a shy, pretty woman who disappears to prepare coffee. Banayout and I sit on a sofa, he turning pages in a photograph album. Here is a sister, who is a singer, in a beautiful velvet dress "made by my father"; and here is Banayout, entering the Roman Catholic Terra Sancta school. It was started during the time the British controlled Palestine, he relates, adding that, although neither of his parents is Roman Catholic, "They both wanted me to have the opportunity of attending Terra Sancta because the Roman Catholics run the best schools in Jerusalem.

"While studying at Terra Sancta, I also worked at a kibbutz called Ramer Rahel, near Jerusalem, setting tables, serving food, and washing dishes. I earned the equivalent of ten dollars a month. I also worked as a cook's helper in a West Jerusalem hotel called Shalom." Of the Jewish people for whom he worked, he says, "They are people. They treated me well. I can never forget that."

Although he has worked eight hours daily in an East Jerusalem restaurant, he made honor grades and learned, in addition to his native Arabic, English, Hebrew, French, and Greek. Now, on a scholarship, he will go to Greece to study engineering.

Like all young Palestinians, Younan understands the vast differences in the mores of his society and American society. "Young people can live together in your country without getting married, but in this country it is a disgrace. If a girl meets a boy, even for a coffee, she can't tell her father because he will break her neck. Here, a man, in order to see a woman, must say he is going to marry her. If he does not, it is difficult to speak to her."

He has a steady girlfriend, and they have no problem seeing each other because he has indicated to both his and her families that once he is established in a job he will marry her. He stresses that he wants to have one woman—not many women.

"Perhaps it is not the way for others. It is for me. If I want a woman to be true to me, what I want her to do, I also must do."

Younan's mother enters the room, serves us coffee, and departs. Younan, who says his mother understands little English, adds that she has not been happy with his determination to go with only one woman. She would prefer his having a wider selection. "And I tried that for awhile. But I felt very sad. And I thought of the Arab proverb, 'The thief is afraid for his home.'

"Everywhere I see men who are wrong, who cheat, steal. I do not try to change anyone. But no one can change me. Always inside I am happy. What will happen to me, I don't care. I want to face any problem. If you have a problem, and you can't solve it, just enjoy it. With any problem, I deal with it and leave it. If not, I will think too much of it."

As we talk, Younan plays records of his favorite music—The Bee Gees and *Saturday Night Fever*, and Vicki Carr singing, "If You Go Away." "I can't live without music," he says. Both Younan and his father play the clarinet.

On a later visit, he relates a difficult problem he has had to settle: the status of his relationship with his girlfriend. "I explained that I would be studying for six or seven years and then we would be married. Meanwhile, I would make a total commitment to her, and she must make a total commitment to me. When I proposed this, asking if she could wait, she hesitated and said she was 'not sure.' I thought about her uncertainty, and then I broke the relationship. I would feel stronger going with her pledge, but I realize it was asking a great deal of her."

The week of his graduation from Terra Sancta, we walk from his home in the Old City to visit the school. Younan continues to talk about his desire for fidelity, saying that when he gets married, "I don't think my wife will cheat on me because I will not cheat on her." His brothers, who are twenty-two and twenty-three, "go with any woman, Arabic, Greek, American, Muslim, Christian, Jew." One brother told him, "I do not believe in love; the woman who at any moment makes me happy—that is love." As we walk in the narrow streets, we seem encapsulated in an Arab world with its special foods, music, smells. We are surrounded by Arab shop owners and, brushing against us, a multitude of other Arabs in long, flowing robes and Arab headgear. They are not Christians but Muslims.

Is there an inner conflict, I ask Younan, in identifying with all that surrounds him, the Arabness of his world that is so overwhelmingly Muslim while also identifying himself as a Christian? What is he first of all? An Arab? A Christian?

"In some instances it is natural to feel a conflict between identifying most of all with your own people, the Arabs, with their traditional social customs and beliefs, and the wider world of the Christian West with its different cultural values," he says. "However, I want and accept both worlds. If you ask if I feel alienated from my Arab world, I will reply that reading and studying, in one sense, alienate a person. If you are born of parents who believe in a fundamentalist concept, you grow beyond that; thus education may alienate you briefly from a secure dogma, but it allows you to find your own certitude."

At Terra Sancta the classrooms are empty; it is the week of graduation. Younan wants to say goodbye to a favorite teacher, named Khader, a native Palestinian in his sixties who has taught school for thirty-three years, is married, with three girls and two boys, and earns the equivalent of three hundred dollars a month.

"I try to teach my students to strive," Khader tells me, as we sit in his office. "However, life for the Palestinians in an occupied land is difficult. We are not living as we should live. We are merely surviving. There are few opportunities for students. Banayout is an exception in that he has a chance to study in Greece. But we are losing our best people; they are all going outside. Because we are not free in our own land."

From the school, we walk back to Younan's home. Along the way, Younan, echoing the sentiments of his teacher, speaks fervently of his desire for the establishment of a Palestine state, and adds that he shares this most cherished aspiration with his Muslim friends. "The common goal of all Palestinians unites us," he says, adding what countless Arabs tell me: "We Arab Muslims and Arab Christians are not different in our basic goal—to live free in our land of Palestine."

Ousama:
Born in a Convent

I first met a young man named Ousama in a Roman Catholic convent within the walls of the Old City. He works at this convent that is called Ecce Homo, a name deriving from the words "Behold the Man" spoken of Christ by the Roman Pontius Pilate.

I lived for some months in Ecce Homo, which, like other convents in the Old City, has rooms for rent. Sister Donna, a slender, attractive, blond Canadian, along with a half-dozen other nuns called the Sisters of Zion, run the convent. Most of the persons who through the decades have worked in the convent and whom Sister Donna hires to work there today are Palestinian Arabs, such as Hilda, her office manager, and Ousama, who serves meals and works behind a cash register in the convent's gift shop.

I choose to write about Ousama, an Arab Muslim, in this section dealing with Christianity, because Ousama—like millions of other Arabs in the Middle East and like millions of Jews in the Western world, especially America—has been influenced by Christianity. They have worked for Christian institutions, attended Christian schools, and knowingly and unknowingly accepted Christian values, which to my mind are not basically different from the good values one also finds in Judaism and Islam.

Someone once said we are a part of all that we have met and known, and Ousama, who is twenty, of medium height, with brown, unruly hair and brown, lively eyes, will always be a part of what he has experienced at the convent. Having an uneven nose and crooked teeth, Ousama was not to my eyes handsome until I came to know his personality. He moves with a quickness in his step that reveals a spirit, a zest for life, and this zest attracts me and others and makes it enjoyable to be in his presence.

71

"You know I was born in this convent," Ousama tells me once when we stand on the terrace of Ecce Homo, enjoying a spectacular sunset. "Everyone knows that nuns generally live in a convent, right? And priests conduct the masses," he continues, with an ironic sense of humor. "But I, an Arab Muslim, am born here!"

He takes my arm and propels me toward a stairway descending to a chapel, and pointing below he explains, "There is a small closet down there." He goes back in time to the Israeli struggle to create a state, when his father's parents were made homeless. His father, Fakhri, then a child of eight, knocked on the door of Ecce Homo, and the Sisters of Zion took him in, allowing him to stay in the "closet" and assigning him such tasks as delivering mail and shopping for fruits and vegetables. Fakhri continued to live in the closet, and when he married he took his thirteen-year-old bride, Ibtissam, to live there. Like most Middle Eastern women of her generation, she was a child bride, who first saw her husband on the day she married him. In that windowless room she gave birth to Natwa, now twenty-two, and to Nahla, now twenty-one, and to Ousama.

Later, Fakhri and his four brothers built a house and all moved into this house with their large and still-growing families. One day, Ousama invites me to his home to share the togetherness of the seventy-six members of his and his uncles' families. Ousama's mother, Ibtissam, a large, happy woman of thirty-six, serves Arab coffee and gives the names of her eight children, starting with Natwa, the eldest, and ending with Rema, four. I sit in a small living room crowded with people and with plants that flourish as in a jungle, and watch the nephews and nieces march in and out of Ousama's arms like armies of ants. While paying attention to each of his nieces and nephews, Ousama talks to me about college.

He explains he could work full-time and go to the small Palestinian university called Bir Zeit, or to the small Roman Catholic Bethlehem University—both are on a par with American junior colleges—or try for the prestigious Hebrew University in Jerusalem, a university built by Jews for Jews. So few Arabs students enter here, an American college professor said, that "it is somewhat the equivalent of a black sharecropper in the 1930s entering Harvard."

Nevertheless, knowing that Hebrew University offers a course in Hebrew—one of five languages he speaks—for "foreigners," and that

this course accepts Europeans and Americans and a few Arabs, usually Arab Jews from Arabic-speaking countries, Ousama presented
himself "as a foreigner." On the basis of his outstanding grades—he
had completed a year at Bethlehem University—he was accepted.

One day I visit the Hebrew University campus with him. He
likes the Jews there, and they like him. Later I visit the Palestinian
Bir Zeit University with him—we go especially to see a mutual
friend, Kareemi—and he introduces me to friends he has known in
Arab elementary and middle schools and at Bethlehem University.
We sit on a bench watching teams from Bethlehem University and
Bir Zeit play soccer, and Ousama talks to me, as Younan had done,
of an alienation that education can bring. He has stepped away or
beyond the close companionship of his former classmates. Except for
a rare occasion, such as our visit to Bir Zeit, he no longer sees them.
He has moved into a higher educational level. He knows that it
means a sacrifice, and he reveals a pain that always goes with growth.

Ousama, it seems to me—and perhaps this has something to do
with his being, in my mind at least, part Muslim but also part Christian and Jew—will always be able to move in any social, economic,
or religious circle and feel himself comfortable there. In a battle
waged between two mortal enemies, he could be dropped from a
high wall and, landing on either side, find himself among friends.

Once Kareemi and Ousama and I meet at Ecce Homo, the convent where they had first come to know each other, having been
invited, individually, to attend a ten-day interfaith seminar there.
They show me the adjoining rooms where they had slept for ten days
in May. Kareemi recalls how each morning Ousama would tap on
the wall of her room and call out, "It's your neighbor's son. Time to
get up!" Kareemi laughs giddily, as though intoxicated by the
remembrance of those days. Each seems guileless, innocent, child-
like. And understanding something of their restrictive culture, I feel
they were not free to go beyond his tapping on the wall.

The three of us walk to the terrace and stand, looking over the
Old City. This was where Kareemi and Ousama had stood when
time had no ballast, and they had discovered how easily, with the
right companion, the night can turn to day. In those days, Kareemi
says, they lived "a time of no time."

We walk out of the convent and into the Via Dolorosa, and years from now, I reflect, Kareemi will remember how we turned left and when we got to a certain shop, Ousama reached into his pocket and, with insouciance, spent a week's wages to buy us souvenirs and sweets. And finally he put us into a taxi, first paying the driver for both of us, and we waved goodbye—to go to the home where Kareemi's mother waited for us.

Some weeks later I encounter Ousama. "Will you go to Bir Zeit? To see Kareemi?" And when I reply that yes, I plan to visit her, he announces with great decisiveness "I am going with you!" My being the intermediary for Ousama makes his visit possible.

Ousama and I ride a bus to Bir Zeit, find Kareemi, and we three then proceed to Kareemi's home in the village of Deir Debwan. Kareemi has telephoned ahead to the village and the neighbors have relayed a message to her mother, who prepares an enormous meal. It is warm enough for us to sit outside, and we eat and laugh and talk for several hours, until the sun goes down. Then Ousama and I leave by bus for Jerusalem. Along the way, he talks:

"All my life I have dreamed of becoming an airline pilot. I see the big planes in the skies that bring visitors to Jerusalem from all parts of the world—and I want to learn to pilot one of the planes." Had Ousama been born in the United States, he would not have dreamed such an impossible dream. But in his land he has no place to go for such studies.

Although Arabs in other countries can get pilot training, Palestinians in the Israeli-occupied West Bank cannot. As a Palestinian, Ousama cannot join the Israeli Air Force for such training. Moreover, Ousama does not want to be a military pilot; he dreams of being a civilian pilot for TWA, Pan-American, or Air France. If Ousama cannot get the training in his home country, why not go outside, say to France? He speaks perfect French and feels an affinity for France. In my enthusiasm, nourished by the limitless opportunities I have had, I urge Ousama to follow his dream. Ousama sighs. The American freedom to travel, to borrow money, and to find a part-time job while pursuing a career—these are realities that millions of Americans take for granted, but to a man without a country and without a passport they are miracles that, through no fault of his own, remain beyond his grasp.

One day I invite Kareemi (who appears again in the Islam segment of this book) to eat with me at the Ecce Homo convent. We are seated at a family-sized table when a nun in habit, who tells us her name is Bernadette and that she is newly arrived from Boston, joins us. Bernadette, sitting next to Kareemi, asks: "Are you a visitor to the Holy Land?" "No," Kareemi replies, "I am a Palestinian."

The American nun is taken aback, confused. Kareemi has named the unnameable. Bernadette, like most Americans, has never met a real live Palestinian. And like most Americans she has perhaps been taught that there are no Palestinian people, only terrorists. Bernadette, who teaches in a secondary school, quickly goes to her heart for a response.

"I know there are good Palestinians just as there are good everybody else. And that a sincere person of any nationality and any faith believes in love." She quotes from an American poet, who said "We must love one another—or die."

However, she continues, "One can't always say in truth 'I love my neighbor.' The best we can do in the beginning is to want to love our neighbor, and I think saying 'I want to love' is more important and more realistic than saying 'I love.'"

Her idea, of course, if that if we say "I *want* to love . . ." often enough, the miracle might occur.

While staying at Ecce Homo convent, I also came to know a Jew now living in Haifa, Israel, who converted to Catholicism and became a priest. He was visiting the convent and told me his story:

"I was born a Jew and converted to Christianity. I became a priest. Since I live in Israel, I requested Israeli authorities to allow me to retain my national identity as a Jew, while at the same time permitting me the freedom to choose my religion. My case went to the Israeli Supreme Court and it ruled that one cannot be a Jew and a Christian. This was an interesting decision because in Israel one has no problem being a Jew and an atheist. In fact, one third of the Israelis are nonbelievers. So a Jew may claim Jewish heritage if he believes in no God, but he cannot claim Jewish heritage if he says I believe in God and in Jesus Christ.

"Actually Israel has many Jews like me, who identify themselves with Christianity. In Haifa, for instance, we regularly hold masses for about two hundred Jews who immigrated to Israel from European countries that were predominantly Catholic. Many young people grew up identifying with Christianity, having gone to Christian schools.

"Some of the young Jews of Christian orientation asked us to intercede on their behalf so they would not have to serve in the Israeli army," the priest continues, "We said no. We believe in a secular state that has a right to its army. But we also believe that within any state, including Israel, one should have religious freedom."

Demetri, a shop owner in the Old City, told me his Christian roots in Jerusalem go back more than four hundred years. "Most of the Christians I know are leaving. And I also will leave. I am leaving because under the Israeli occupation of East Jerusalem we must deal in Israeli currency, and they have an inflation running one hundred fifty percent. Taxes and living costs have gone sky high, but the value of the Israeli currency keeps falling," Demetri said.

Christian Arab families have a lower rate of births than Muslim Arabs, but it is their continuing emigration—for religious, educational, and economic reasons—that most of all threatens the future of the Christian Arab community in the Holy Land.

Accompanied by Ann, a nun born in Hawaii, I go to a 7:00 A.M. mass in the Church of the Holy Sepulcher.

We stand briefly in the courtyard. I want to appreciate this edifice, called the greatest shrine in all Christendom. It is a sprawling construction that has been built and destroyed and rebuilt and enlarged so often I hardly know where to look for beauty or for the aspect that will awe or inspire or make me closer to the Eternal.

Since Byzantine times the Church of the Holy Sepulcher has been the most significant Christian edifice in Jerusalem. It was erected by the Emperor Constantine after his mother, Helena, came to Jerusalem and said she had discovered the sepulcher of Christ and also the Cross on which he died.

In the center of its entrance hall, a flight of steps descends to a chapel named after Helena, and another flight of steps descends to the spot where, we are told, she found the True Cross, the site of the Crucifixion—Golgotha or Calvary. The golden-domed rotunda contains what is said to be the Holy Sepulcher—the burial site of Christ.

In the early mass, Sister Ann and I are among a wide variety of worshipers—Armenians, Greek Orthodox, Roman Catholics, Copts from Egypt—all singing and chanting. As we leave the shrine, Sister

Ann remarks, "It was too noisy! It seemed to be a contest who could sing the loudest."

Although Armenians, Copts, and Roman Catholics share the famed shrine, it traditionally has been a Greek Orthodox Church. To learn more about its history, I seek out a Greek architect-engineer named Paris Papathedorou sent from Athens to supervise repairs on the church. I find his offices within the sacred edifice itself.

"The head of the Greek Orthodox church is called the patriarch, and the Greek Orthodox is the oldest of all the Christian churches," he explains. "Our patriarchate in Jerusalem traces its lineage back to the Council of Chalcedon. That was in the year 451. So we have sixteen hundred years of Greek patriarchy here. The Roman Catholic patriarchate was not founded until 1099, following the conquest of the Holy Land by the first Crusaders. Once we had a large Greek Christian community living in Jerusalem, but after the creation of a Jewish state in 1948, with Christianity no longer the official religion, everything changed. Many Greek Christians left in 1948 and even more after the war of 1967, when the Israelis began their occupation of East Jerusalem. Now we have only two hundred fifty Greek Christians left."

In Bethlehem
with Mervat

Mervat, mentioned earlier, is a young Arab Christian with six brothers and sisters who have left the Holy Land. She herself is torn as to whether to go or stay.

The youngest of eight children born to a Bethlehem stonecutter named Nestas and his wife, Milia, Mervat is soft and plump, not fat, but at seventeen she seems still to be growing out as well as up. She has dark eyes and black hair that curls at her shoulders. Often, when she is displeased with the inequalities of life, her lower lip protrudes in a little pout. Then she looks quite serious, her demeanor indicating that if she but thinks hard enough, she will rectify the wrongs of this world.

Mervat comes from a long-established Christian family, her Christian roots going back, she says, "about seventeen hundred years, to the time of Constantine." She and her family are among the approximately five million Christians who live today in the Middle East. The overwhelming majority of these Christians are not Westerners from Europe or America but Arabs, such as Mervat's family.

I came to know Mervat and her Arab Christian family quite by accident. The story of my coming to know them begins in Jerusalem, and a visit with a tourist group to the Church of the Holy Sepulcher. Leaving the group, I walked through an open courtyard and watched a group of stone masons who were chipping at large and beautiful blocks of stone. I left the church, but the picture of the stones and the stonecutters remained in my mind, and each day for several weeks I returned to stand and watch them at their work. The sight of stonecutters working at Christendom's holiest shrine enabled me to think beyond the conflicts of the present. Temples, fortresses, cathedrals, shrines, mosques, empires, all crumble. And new builders patiently gather and refashion the stones. The hard, ancient, enduring mezzo-stones are solid beauty. They speak of a life before and of a time to come.

Without ever having exchanged any words, I felt I began to know the stonecutters. And as the weeks pass, I learn from Luis, an Arab policeman who guards the shrine, that one of the men has worked at the shrine for eighteen years and that he comes from a long line of stonecutters and "is considered one of the best sculptors in Palestine." I began talking with this man and learn his name—Cirres Elias Nestas. He is short, with graying hair and eyes that fasten on me like a clasp. His eyes seem to say, "You meet a man who knows his worth." He is neither arrogant nor supercilious; rather he conveys the quiet self-confidence of a man who works with his hands and who knows that what he does is good.

Nestas invites me to visit his home. The following Sunday I take a bus from the Damascus Gate in Jerusalem, and twenty minutes later, halfway to Bethlehem, I get off and walk to a nearby house made of white native stone. Nestas' wife, Milia, who is built on a frame with big bones but no fat, greets me. She is tall and strong, energetic, vivacious—a happy woman except when she thinks of the scattering of her children, six of them in other countries and only Mervat and Sami, twenty-six, who studied art and sculpturing in Italy, still at home.

"For hundreds of years, the men in my family have been stonecutters," Nestas tells me when we sit at supper. "We have always worked in the Christian churches, repairing such shrines as the Holy Sepulcher in Jerusalem and the Church of the Nativity in Bethlehem and sculpturing new works of art.

"All my forebears were born and grew up in Bethlehem when it was a Christian town," Nestas continues. "I grew up during the period when Palestine was under the British mandate and Christianity was the official religion. Everyone observed Sunday as a legal holiday—all the shops, schools, and banks were closed."

Nestas was twenty and Milia was thirteen when on Christmas Day, 1943, they were married in the Church of the Nativity in Bethlehem. "In those days we planned our big events around big events, such as a marriage on Christmas," Milia explains.

"I had always known her. We were second cousins," Nestas says,

"We lived here in this house—in our Palestine. Then in 1948, when I was twenty-five, Western powers moved to create a state for the Jews who were coming in from Europe. At this time Jerusalem was fifty percent Christian and Bethlehem was ninety percent Christian. Christians began to leave. The Jews wanted an all-Jewish state, with Judaism as the official religion. Here on the West Bank, after the Israelis began their military occupation over us, the official holidays became Friday and Saturday. Now unless you work for a Christian institution, you find Sunday is like any other work day. This change might seem like a simple one, but for Christians who must work on Sunday it takes a great deal of meaning out of Christianity.

"Steadily, since the creation of a Jewish state, the Arab Christians have been moving out. They are moving out of Bethlehem, Nazareth, Jerusalem—from all over the West Bank and Gaza as well as from Israel. The Jews encourage this exodus. Many Jews say their aim is to rid Palestine of all the Palestinians, the Christians as well as Muslims. The Christians we know who are leaving are educated and do not want to work and live under Jewish domination. There is little for them to do here. We cannot lead our own lives here. About one hundred thousand Christians have moved out since the Jewish occupation began in 1967. Today, Christians represent no more than ten percent of Jerusalem and for that matter, no more than ten percent of all the Holy Land."

I first see Bethlehem with Mervat at my side. From her house it is about two miles to Bethlehem, and we could have walked, but Mervat and her family are modern and seldom do that. Besides, we are in a desert region, and the noonday heat is oppressive. So we board a dilapidated bus with an Arab driver and filled with Arab men, women, and children.

I see the dryness and barrenness and feel the heat. And I think of all the snow in our Christmas cards. The bus turns a corner, and I see at close range the little town with its small, white stone houses nestling in rugged confidence on the Judean hills.

Legend tells us that shepherds were tending their flocks and saw a star and said to one another, let us follow that star to see where it leads us, and it led them to the manger where the Christ child lay. The three religions that have had the most profound influence on the present civilization of the world sprang from the hearts of shepherds, peasants, and caravan men of the Semitic race—that is, people who spoke a Semitic language. Since the story of the shepherds following the star originated, millions of people have followed their own star to the little town of Bethlehem, and until now it has somehow managed to survive with some simplicity.

Tens of millions of devout believers revere this little town. Its meaning in our lives—not only in the lives of Americans but also of Africans, Argentines, Australians, of people in every land of this globe—wells within me.

I turn to Mervat, who is studying a display window with jeans. She once said she thought she understood Americans, but I wonder if she can visualize our celebration of the birth of Christ and the American idea of her town. I tell her that everyone in America knows about Bethlehem. She makes no reply.

I try to explain that we give gifts and build replicas of the Bethlehem manger and sing music about his birth. Instinctively I softly begin to sing:

> O little town of Bethlehem
> How still we see thee lie,
> Above thy deep and dreamless sleep
> The silent stars go by;
> Yet in thy dark streets shineth . . .

We sing that song in America, I tell Mervat.

"It sounds rather silly," Mervat responds. She asks me about the meaning of a "deep and dreamless sleep." Those words make Bethlehem sound unreal to her. Her town is a place where she goes to school, meets her friends, and shops for jeans. "We never sing such songs," she says, with a shrug of her shoulders. Mervat causes me wonder. What kind of Christian is she, anyway, if she doesn't know our songs?

We see towers, domes, steeples of dozens of Christian churches. Mervat points out Christian convents, hospitals, orphanages, schools. Most of these, including Bethlehem University, are run by Roman Catholic priests and nuns from America and Europe.

"That is the school I attend," and Mervat points to a distant two-story stone building called the Good Shepherds School, named for the field two miles east of Bethlehem where tradition tells us shepherds on the night of Christ's birth guarded their sheep. The school is run by Swedish Protestants.

"Families who can afford to do so always send their children to a Christian school. Most schools in Bethlehem are Roman Catholic, but all the Christian schools are good. For one reason, the Christian schools are less crowded.

"You may find sixty or more students in a public school classroom, but only thirty in a Christian school. You can talk to the teachers, and if you need help they will have time to help you. The teachers are well trained, and you move along faster than in the public schools.

"All Christian schools accept both Arab Muslims as well as Arab Christians. As a rule, however, not as many Muslim parents send their children to Christian schools as Arab Christian parents do," Mervat says, pointing out again that, while Christianity sprang from her homeland in the East, it moved westward, adopting the Western belief in the importance of universal education.

"My Muslim friends have not been in school as long as I," Mervat observes, although, she adds, "they are just as smart."

We leave the Arab bus near a large paved courtyard filled with tourist buses bringing visitors from every corner of the globe to Bethlehem. In the streets we meet many of her schoolmates, wearing skintight blue jeans, blouses and high heels. Old women wear the traditional long black dress with a colorfully embroidered bodice, a dress that is seen only in Bethlehem. Strolling through the town, I notice store signs in English as well as Arabic. But I do not see any sign in Hebrew.

"This is a Palestinian town," Mervat reminds me. "No Jews live here. The only Jews are the soldiers. Look at them on the roofs of the buildings. They are everywhere. They stop you. You have to answer their silly questions. And they arrest whomever they please, women or men."

Mervat is en route to her school and she now waves goodbye to me. I cross Manger Square—it is a paved courtyard, with a fountain designed by Mervat's father and brother Sami—and I enter a low, small door leading into the Church of the Nativity, said to be the oldest Christian church, and go down to the very spot, so we are told, where Christ was born. It is marked by the design of a star set in the stone floor. A few Arab Christians are standing, with heads bowed in prayer. They make the Sign of the Cross and leave. A black man about thirty, dressed in a new suit that looks as if it were made in America, lights a candle and leaves it in a candelabra. Then he bends over the site of the star in the stone floor, kisses the star, and leaves.

I am seated on a narrow bench near a young man in a long black frock coat. He has dirty blond hair and a beard and the Christlike face we see in cheap stereotype paintings. He and I sit quietly for about ten minutes. When he leaves, I read "Liquor is the root of all evil" printed on the back of his coat. A woman about fifty, with a red-and-white-striped pantsuit, oversized handbag, and husband and guide in tow, descends the steps.

"*Is that it?*" she asks in a loud voice, pointing to the star on the floor.

"Yes," the guide replies, "The star indicates the spot. And over there"—and he points some four or five feet to another recess carved in the wall—"is the manger."

"Oh," says the woman. "I thought he was born in the manger."

"No. He was born where the star is, and then she put him *there*" —and he points to the second niche. "There were some caves here, natural grottos," he continues.

"But," interrupts the woman, "I thought he was born in a manger."

"Yes, yes," he says, "but it wasn't a manger as you know it; it was more like a cave."

After snapping her picture by the exact spot, he escorts her and her husband up the steps.

I, too, leave the site of the manger and ascend the steps. As I walk out the small entrance door of the shrine, I encounter a group with a guide who wears a yarmulke, or skullcap. Are they a Jewish group? I ask their guide.

"Yes," he replies. "We are Jews from Australia." As they enter, one by one, through the narrow door, I overhear an Australian Jewish mother tell her daughter, about eight, "This is where Jesus was born."

"Was he born in this church?" the child asks.

"No," replies the mother, irritated, "I have told you three times already he was born in a manger."

I cannot blame the mother for being confused. The church does not look like a manger.

I wait outside the church, and soon the Australian Jews finish their tour. As they file out, I approach an Australian man, about sixty, and after identifying myself I ask him how he is enjoying his tour of the Holy Land.

"To my surprise, I have identified with the Christian shrines more than with the Jewish ones," the Australian tells me, apparently glad to have someone share his thoughts. I had heard the same statement made by a New York editor of Jewish heritage. Each explained that he came from a nation that is called Christian, and the New Yorker, as well as the Australian, said, "I became a part of the predominant culture."

I return on several occasions to the Church of the Nativity with Mervat. It is not a tourist attraction for her, but a shrine where she and her family worship, where her mother and father were married, and where her eldest brother, Fakhre, now living in Houston, Texas, was married.

One day we experience a kind of miracle. We find ourselves alone in the shrine, all the tourists, for the moment at least, having departed. I experience the immensity of the church and the individual struggle to give a worthwhile meaning to one's life.

Mervat takes small coins from a pocket. She leaves the coins in a money box, takes two candles, and hands one to me, saying that when we light our candles, "We can make a wish." We close our eyes, make our wishes, and, leaving the candles on a candelabra, walk from the darkened interior into the heat and intensity of the Mediterranean sun.

"What did you wish?" Mervat asks. I say that I prayed or wished to be fair to everyone. Mervat is simpler. She says she wishes to be my friend.

Once in the Church of the Nativity, Mervat and I find ourselves amid thirty or forty young American men dressed in civilian clothes. One volunteers that they are sailors from a United States ship that docked that week at an Israeli port.

"Look at this detail, look at this detail," one sailor notes of the ornamentations in the shrine that serves both the Greek Orthodox and Roman Catholic communities.

"I wish they had left it natural, without all that stuff," another sailor observes, meaning the small lanterns, candles, and other religious objects.

Mervat and I join the Americans and we all descend the narrow steps to the replica of the manger.

We linger near the sailors to overhear their guide explain that a certain Justin Martyr, "a native of Palestine," proclaimed in the middle of the second century that Christ was born in a cave near Bethlehem. The guide does not elaborate on how Justin Martyr knew where Christ was born.

"Some three hundred years after Christ was born, the Emperor Constantine saw a message in the sky. He saw the cross and the words, 'In this sign, conquer,'" the guide relates.

"Having seen this sign, Constantine then sent his mother, Queen Helena, to the Holy Land to build shrines to Christ. Helena commissioned the building of this church on the site where Christ was born, as well as a church on the Mount of Olives, where Jesus prayed, and the Church of the Holy Sepulcher in Jerusalem.

"Although the two churches Queen Helena commissioned in Jerusalem were destroyed and rebuilt, this church has remained until now—the oldest church in the world.

"Christ spent three years in his ministry, and so far as we know, he never wrote his thoughts. We derive our knowledge of the life of Christ from four short interpretations called Gospels, and from a few other New Testament references to him," the guide says. "With only a few historical references to Jesus Christ, writers have written more books about him than about anyone who ever lived.

"Paul the Apostle wrote the first Christian literature. But, as far as we know, he never saw Christ in the flesh. Until the time of Constantine there were few Christians. Now Christianity has more followers than any other religion in the world."

Returning home, again by Arab bus, Mervat and I pass a Palestinian refugee camp called Dahisha.

"You see the refugees, the poorest of the poor—and look what is next door to us." Then Mervat points across the ancient landscape to a scene that to her eyes must seem a mirage. Tens of dozens of tall, modern, massive stone skyscrapers that overwhelm her sense of proportion, and in their numbers and immensity threaten to obliterate her "little town" of Bethlehem and her way of life as well.

"Just two kilometers from my home," Mervat says of the new

Jewish colony called Gilo built illegally on Arab land. I ask her how many will live here.

She asks me to estimate. I study the skyscrapers and guess thirty, fifty thousand—maybe one hundred thousand.

"All built with money from America," Mervat adds.

Every Palestinian I met understands that such settlements, which the United States government says are illegal, are nevertheless built with money from America. Altogether the United States has sent Israel more than twenty-three billion dollars.

Mervat says she finds it difficult to accept the reality of the Jewish settlement. "I think it is something I am seeing on a screen, in a movie," she says.

Does she ever talk to any Jewish people?

"Jewish people?" she repeats. "No." She never sees them as individuals. Not in her school, nor when she shops. She sees only the Jewish soldiers. And the huge complex of housing units. The Jewish colonists have their own special buses that take them to and from their settlement into Jerusalem. And, as yet, "they never shop in Bethlehem."

Getting off the bus, Mervat and I walk a short distance to a two-story stone house and ring a bell. Mervat's cousin, Suzy, also seventeen, opens the door. Doll-sized, with long, dark hair, Suzy studies at a Roman Catholic school run by French Catholic teachers. She speaks Arabic, French, English, and Hebrew. Mervat speaks Arabic, French, English, some German, some Italian, and some Hebrew.

"I study diligently, and I feel myself different from my classmates. For the most, if a man wants to marry them, then they will marry," Suzy says.

Does she date? "No, it is forbidden. But Mervat and I often go to parties, to celebrate birthdays or family parties, as when someone gets a new house. Or we go disco dancing. And our parents are also there."

We sit in Suzy's bedroom, listening to an Arab radio station that spins out first Arabic, then American music. We listen to "Lady in Blue" and "I'll Put You Together Again." Mervat and Suzy both know all the popular stateside tunes.

And what do the girls want to be? "A medical doctor of dentistry," Mervat replies.

And Suzy?

"An engineer."

Knowing how important having a heroine or a model is for young women, I ask if Suzy knows any woman engineer.

"Yes. We have a woman engineer in Bethlehem. She is the first. She is from France."

And does Mervat know a woman dentist?

"Yes, my cousin in Bethlehem. Her husband is a medical doctor, and my cousin trained as a dentist in Damascus."

"I feel equal with a man," Suzy says in a soft, yet determined voice. Perhaps her mother and grandmother had that same feeling, but then no woman in her family ever went as far in her education as has Suzy. None of them dreamed of going to college, even to study cooking, much less engineering. And certainly none of them ever gave a thought to dressing and acting like a man. They lived in a different world from Suzy and Mervat.

When they discuss religion or politics, the girls seem older than their years. They are a contrast to American high school boys and girls I have known who are no longer involved in political issues as much as they were in the sixties.

"The Israelis deport our leaders, but we will grow up and be leaders," Mervat says. The girls are growing up amid violent forces, and they feel a part of those forces. Nationalism is part of the air one breathes in the occupied West Bank.

Mervat and Suzy are entering the stream of women around the world who are stepping out of the typical feminine role. They no longer want only to cook and wash and sew. They want the same education and job opportunities as men. In the Arab world, this is revolutionary.

In their liberated ways, they are far removed from many of their countrywomen, but even so, Mervat continues many societal traditions—patterns that are prevalent and deeply ingrained and expressed with love and devotion, but nevertheless designed to indicate man is number one and woman is number two. For example, once I ask Mervat to name her brothers and sisters, and she names Fakhre and Fawssi and Sami, "and these are the men." Then she proceeds to name the women: Ellen, Nadia, Nahad, and Nawal. Ellen, I learn, is older than Fakhre, but in Mervat's society one does not name the firstborn child first if she is a female. Rather, one names the first male child and then the other male children and after all the male children are named, one then lists the female offspring.

Once I ask Mervat's mother what was her happiest time.

"When my son was born," she replies without hesitation.

She had first given birth to Ellen. Why was not that her happiest moment?

"You and your husband are given a second name when you give birth to a son," she explains. I knew, for example that in the case of Nestas everyone who worked at the Church of the Holy Sepulcher called him the father of Fakhre—abu Fakhre.

"It is tradition. And so a woman is most happy to be able to honor her husband by giving birth to a son," Milia said.

I try to visualize the woman sitting before me as a thirteen-year-old bride. I suggest to Milia what I've heard: it is better to have children when you are young.

"I had no way of planning. The babies kept coming," she replies with a laugh.

The typical Palestinian family is large—perhaps ten, twelve, even up to nineteen members. The Jewish people have become alarmed by the large growth rate of Palestinians. They are fearful that the Arabs within the Israeli-occupied territories will outnumber them. But studies throughout the world indicate that as families gain upward mobility, stepping out of the poverty level, they want more clothes, cars, radios and TVs, and fewer children. Mervat, for example, says she plans to have no children. She does not think it possible to marry in her Arab world and retain a sense of freedom and to work creatively, and thus she builds an armor around herself by declaring "I hate men" and "I will never marry." Or, "I do not want to spend my time thinking about men" and "A woman needs to be more than a housekeeper." She bypasses Egyptian movies when they are shown in Bethlehem because "they are only about love and marriage."

Once at home we listen to a very popular Egyptian singer, Farid al-Atraash, who conveys a tone of anguish.

What is she saying? I ask.

"Oh, she is in love," Mervat replies in disgust.

Mervat flips off the radio and turns on TV. It is time for the

American serial, "Little House on the Prairie," which is Milia's favorite. And what is Mervat's favorite?

"'Roots' is my favorite of any TV production," she replies. Her other favorites include "Space in 1999," "Rich Man, Poor Man," old Charlie Chaplin films, "Blake," "Peyton Place," "Steve Halston," and "Enterprise." Her brother Sami prefers TV "mysteries and thrillers," while her father likes all sports, especially boxing and soccer.

Each evening at the Nestas home we watch the news. "Israel has censorship, so the Tel Aviv station reports only censored news. But luckily, we can tune into Jordan, as well as Lebanon, Syria, and Cyprus," Nestas explains. We watch an hour of news emanating from a station in Amman, Jordan, and a half hour of news emanating from a Tel Aviv station. Jordanian TV carries a news program in Hebrew, while Israel carries a news program in Arabic. We see only one bilingual program: an Israeli cooking show that lists the ingredients in both Hebrew and Arabic.

"All the situation comedies we watch are produced in America," Nestas says. "They are written and produced by Americans who practice the reverse of anti-Semitism, which is anti-Arabism. They are clever at creating propaganda: in their films they are telling millions of viewers that we Arabs are cruel, primitive, greedy. They make us all into one stereotype who wears a moustache, dark glasses, has a hooked nose, and is a terrorist. In 'Angels on Ice' we see Arab assassins. In 'The Six Million Dollar Man' we watch an Arab diplomat conduct blackmail. In 'Police Woman' and 'McCloud' my people abduct young girls for enslavement. In 'Hawaii Five-O' Arabs are arrogant, and a dog is called 'Muhammad.' Yet I doubt that American producers would film a show in which someone would say, 'Hey, Christ', when calling a dog.

"We Arabs are a hundred million people—we do not all wear dark glasses, leer, and act fiendish. We do not all own oil wells and throw bombs. We do not all bow to Muhammad. We also are Arab Christians, and Arab Jews. Television ignores our reality. In the made-in-America TV productions, I have never seen a human Arab, a good Arab. I have never seen an Arab hero."

On a Christmas Eve Mervat and I sit talking in the small bedroom that is separated by curtain from the living-dining area. Mervat's father and mother and brother Sami are hammering and nailing. In modernizing the small house they themselves have installed plumbing, electricity, and gas. About 8:00 P.M., Sami stops work and goes in his 1941 Chevrolet to shop for meat, onions, and green peppers. On his return he and his father gather olive wood and build an outdoor fire. Mervat and I, being cold inside the unheated house, go outdoors by the blazing fire. We watch as Sami cuts the pork, placing small chunks, along with chopped onions and peppers, on skewers. Once the fire is reduced to simmering coals, he places the pork kebab over the coals.

"We eat pork every Christmas. Christians can eat pork, but Muslims and Jews cannot," Mervat explains. "Each Christmas we cook outdoors under the stars. The custom started with the shepherds. They were out in the fields at night. And this is the way they must have cooked their meal the night before Jesus was born."

As we stand around the fire, I see the lights of Bethlehem in the distance. Also, on the nearby highway, I see a stream of Israeli buses and Israeli taxis and private cars, whose drivers have special permits to enter Bethlehem during the Christmas season.

What, I ask Mervat, does she think being Christian means?

"I think it means being able to forgive. You can forgive your enemy and build anew," she replies, with no hesitation.

Nestas looks pleased with his daughter's reply. He adds there is not enough "forgiving" in the Middle East today.

The next day, Christmas, Mervat and I walk from her home toward Bethlehem. I am appalled by the number of soldiers I see all around us—more soldiers perhaps than I have ever seen outside war maneuvers. The soldiers have sealed off the town. It looks as if it is under siege.

Along the road leading into town, Mervat and I are stopped a half dozen times. Mervat wisely carries nothing in her hands, but I have a large purse and each time we are stopped I must show not only my passport but each item in my purse. On Christmas Day little or no traffic is permitted inside the town, so the only vehicles we see moving are jeeps with Israeli soldiers. We see soldiers on all the rooftops, standing feet apart, with binoculars to their faces and guns slung over their shoulders.

"We get used to them. I have always seen them at Christmas. They have charge of our Christmas program. They organize the coming and going of all pilgrims and visitors. A Christmas without the Jewish soldiers all over our town would hardly seem like Christmas. I have seen them every year since I was four." Mervat, who was born in 1963, says.

We are soon inside Bethlehem, among thousands of native Palestinian Arabs and visiting pilgrims, from all corners of the globe, all of us squeezed together and snaking forward.

I stand on tiptoes and see newly erected wooden cubicles that are designated for men and women, with signs in English as well as in Arabic. Why, I ask Mervat, are so many people waiting to get inside? Are they public toilets?

"No," she replies with a bitter laugh. "They are security checkpoints. Everyone entering Bethlehem to celebrate Christmas must be frisked." A young Swedish pilgrim with a knapsack asks Mervat in English: "Who guarded Manger Square before the occupation?"

"I guess God," Mervat replies.

Waiting—we are now behind an iron barricade—I meet an American, Dr. Howatt E. Mallinson, who for twenty-six years was pastor of the Whythe Presbyterian Church in Hampton, Virginia. He observes, "Bethlehem today must be very much like it was two thousand years ago when Roman soldiers were in charge," he observes. Then he adds, "It is a sad scene. I would not want to return to Bethlehem, not as long as it is under military occupation."

Mervat, in front of me, enters a booth, and after she has been inspected I enter and an Israeli woman soldier runs her hands over my body to ascertain that I do not carry weapons. Leaving the booths, Mervat and I proceed to Manger Square. Eventually we station ourselves amid a throng of perhaps twenty thousand pilgrims facing the square, which is about the size of a basketball court. Israeli uniformed armed soldiers and high-ranking officers talk into their walkie-talkies and briskly pace the courtyard checking details. Overhead, Israeli jets streak across a clear sky. After the jets come helicopters. The fair-skinned soldiers of Western descent, center stage, welcome the Palestinian mayor of Bethlehem to his hometown, and they greet the Church dignitaries, who wear long impressive robes and hats. The Israeli soldiers instruct the Christians how to march in their procession. Of the Israeli military Mervat observes, "They think it is their Christmas."

Suddenly Mervat feels faint, and falls against me. "I can't breathe." At the same moment, we hear voices—"He's coming. He's coming!"—and a roll of drums.

Holding on to Mervat, I attempt to move her out for air. Meanwhile, the Greek patriarch riding in a white Mercedes, escorted by Jewish soldiers on white horses, arrives at Manger Square. Mervat is too ill to look. I get her to an iron barricaded gate guarded by an Israeli soldier.

She's ill, I tell him.

"You cannot leave now," he asserts, in English. Then he gives Mervat a compassionate look and allows us to pass.

Once in open space Mervat feels better. We walk slowly back home and rest.

The previous evening I had gone alone to Bethlehem to the Church of the Nativity for the midnight mass that is televised around the world. The white altar was covered with white linen and was bare save for a vase filled with red roses. The mass began with Scripture from the Apostle Paul, urging that we have "no ambition except to do good," read in several languages, including French, Arabic, and English. A young man on my right, perhaps twenty-three, volunteers he is from Los Angeles; then he closes his eyes and seemingly transports himself to another world. A Roman Catholic nun, on my left, silently sheds tears. Nearby, an American couple from Nebraska, wanting to share this special moment, lean over and in a whisper say they had saved twenty-five years for this night in Bethlehem.

In looking over the audience—the vast majority white visitors from America and Europe—I am surprised to find a face I know, a Roman Catholic nun, Angela Erevia, from my native state of Texas. After the mass I find her, and we chat briefly and arrange to meet the following day in Jerusalem. She relates her impressions of spending the Christian holy days in a Jewish state.

"First, I learned that being in West Jerusalem at Christmas is nothing like our idea of Christmas. West Jerusalem is of course all Jewish and the banks and stores stay open on Christmas Day, so it is like any other day of the week. I have not heard 'Jingle Bells' or

'I'm Dreaming of a White Christmas.' I have not seen Christmas trees nor felt the excitement of shopping, or exchanging cards and gifts and going to parties. Since there is nothing externally in West Jerusalem to remind you of Christmas, you must make it an internal experience. I remind myself I made an external 'pilgrimage'—coming to the Holy Land. Then, going into Bethlehem, I was angered by seeing so many hundreds of Israeli soldiers who were constantly checking my possessions and running their hands over my body. Then I decided, externally these people can check me. Internally I will check myself.

"I had time to reflect on Jesus. I was able to see him as a solitary figure, yet with a power within Him to transform people. This gave me peace. I transformed the annoying experience into a prayer experience."

One day, Mervat leads me up one of the hills on which Bethlehem has grown, and we enter the small campus of Bethlehem University, run by the Roman Catholic Church.

Palestinian Arab students, young women as well as men, are gathered in a courtyard between classes. Mervat and I climb steps to the offices of the head of the university, Brother Joseph Lowenstein.

We do not have an appointment, but we talk with a secretary who sends us to a reception room. After a brief wait, the secretary takes us to the office of Brother Lowenstein. We walk in and shake hands with a pleasant man in his middle years. He motions us to chairs in front of his desk and, at my request, he begins with a short resume of his life.

"I was born in New York and I belong to an order called the Christian Brothers, probably best known in America for its wine. This is an international order, with its main headquarters in Rome. We opened Bethlehem University, which is Vatican endowed and subsidized, in 1973 with eighty students. Now it has six hundred twenty-five students, one-third women. While this is a Christian university, we welcome Muslims as well as Christian Arabs. The Muslim Arab students here now outnumber the Christian Arabs. They have no problems among themselves. Arab Christian and Arab Muslim students live and attend classes together. They all study certain topics of the Koran as well as the Bible, and you see them rubbing elbows and discussing aspects of Islam and Christianity on an intellectual plane. The story of Jesus, including the virgin birth and ascension, is in the Koran.

"Arab Christians and Arab Muslims are closer here in Palestine than in any other place in the Middle East. This is because the Israeli occupation has made second-class citizens of all Palestinian Arabs, Christians as well as Muslims. Here, both Muslims and Christians are oppressed. The Israeli soldiers have on many occasions stormed our campus. They break into our classrooms and arrest our students. Of course the students demonstrate against the Israeli occupation. Anyone, of any creed or nationality, would. You cannot have an oppressed society without expecting students to react.

"We know that America gives money to support the continual takeover of Arab land in Jerusalem, Gaza, and the West Bank. And I feel guilty about this, a guilt of silence, of compliance.

"For years we kept silent in America about our racism. Now I see an analogy between how we treated blacks and how white European Israelis treat Palestinians. Until I came here, I could never have dreamed a racism like this could exist in the Holy Land, but if you live here awhile you see it and it becomes a fact you are forced to recognize.

"We Christians of the West have not taken a moral stand. We have spoken for justice for other peoples, but not for the Palestinians. Those of us who live here know the suffering of the Palestinians, and we must have the courage to speak for that suffering. Moreover, a claim to Palestine must be based on the realities of the twentieth century without reference to a history that took place several millennia ago."

Brother Joseph adds that it is the teachings of a militant Zionism that cause the Israelis to confiscate lands and torture innocent people. "And this political creed of militant Zionism is the negation of Christianity."

Sometime after Mervat and I visited Bethlehem University. a young Palestinian woman student at the university, Taghrid Butmma, nineteen, was shot by Israeli border police—"accidentally" according to the Israeli officials, and "deliberately" according to her friends.

"No Palestinian believes it was an accident," Mervat said. "We

believe they would like to kill us all. That is why we grow angry
and resist their oppression." She sighed and then turned to a Palestinian poet to sum up her feelings:

> I am . . .
> Against the rose-beds turning to trenches . . .
> And yet
> When fire cremates my friends
> > my youth
> > and my country
> How can I
> Stop a poem from becoming a gun?

JUDAISM
CHRISTIANITY
ISLAM

The Old Walled City:
Arab East Jerusalem

Mahmud ali Hassan is a beautiful old Arab, with a kind face and soft, brown eyes, and for a moment I thought I perceived the history of this land written in his face. He is a sculptor, a restorer of mosaics and shards, an archaeologist, courtly in manners. And yet he reveals a spirit that has been broken—perhaps by wanting to love others as much as his art and not finding this possible.

I came to feel close to him, and he showed me "the holiest place in the world"—the area of the Temple Mount, the site the Jews call their Rock Moriah, over which the Muslims built their magnificent Dome of the Rock and al-Aqsa Mosque. One day we walked the alleyways of the Old City, and on another day, he guided me through the Rockefeller Museum, formerly called the Palestine Museum, which he was instrumental in creating. I had thought we were friends—and then it was all over. I reached out to touch him, and he was not there.

I cannot say, Hassan, what happened? In his culture he would think (as I have thought at times about a person in another culture), if she does not know, if she is so obtuse as not to understand, then all I can say will not penetrate. As for me, the nuances are there, and I am pained by much that I understand and by all I do not understand.

I would like to pretend that I did not know what happened. But I saw what happened. The day that Hassan and I came out of the Rockefeller Museum he saw at a side door some old Arab friends, who continue to work as guards, and he excused himself to greet them, reentering the museum. I stood in the shade of a tree, and a young, handsome man with fair skin, light hair, and blue eyes approached and began talking. I did not think or care in those moments who he was—archaeologist, salesman, or tourist, Christian, Muslim, or Jew. But as he seemed eager for a new friend, I responded in kind, and as we chatted I learned he was an Israeli Jew whose family had immigrated from South Africa. He volunteered his name and said he would like to visit me. We were exchanging small slips of paper with names and addresses when Hassan came out the door.

Seeing Hassan approach us, I noted his usual gentle features freeze into a rigidity, a mixture, I thought, of fear and hate. I saw him change from a person I knew to a person I did not know. My mind would not accept that, so I dismissed the thought, the idea. Yet when I attempted to introduce Hassan to my new acquaintance, the old Arab looked past him, would not acknowledge him.

I reassured myself that he and I were still friends. But as Hassan and I walked away, his silence communicated that he was not really there; a stone statue walked beside me. I searched for an excuse, a reason, some logical explanation. I recalled to mind what a school-teacher, an Arab, had once said to me, "They are Jews, we are Arabs, and we are enemies."

I had been mixing among my Jewish friends, then among my Arab friends. But never with both Arabs and Jews.

But as to Hassan's breaking our friendship over my brief moment in the presence of a Jew, my mind still refused to accept that. Yet my heart knew that he and I were as finished as if we had been lovers and he, insanely possessive, had found me in the embrace of another man.

The next morning I went, as I often did, to his office in the Islamic Museum and held out my hand in greeting. He would not give his hand. Without looking at me, he said he was "too busy" to visit. I remained standing, my extended hand a plea for mercy and understanding, but I could not enter his heart; he would not raise his arm. Eventually, to assure me, if I needed further assurance, that he wanted no part of what I was offering, he limply raised his left arm and extended a flexed left hand, so all I could touch was an unwilling wrist.

The trust, like some fragile butterfly I might want to hold, to keep forever, had flown out the window. Now I am left only with the good that we shared, the life he had shown me.

Perhaps I cared for him, even "loved" him because he was Hassan. Someone once said that love is a kind of pity. And why should I have pitied old Hassan? He had lived his life and had suffered, which is the lot of any man. The remnants of his Arabic past—when his forebears ruled half the known world—lay in the recessed corners of his life, and he, I thought, nursed those recesses like a dog licks its wounds.

The greatest tragedy in his life was that he, as head of a large family, could not have his children around him, for they were scattered, unable to return to the land where they had been born, a homeland he still calls Palestine. Now he was like King Lear, who no longer had his gold, and worse, no longer had the wealth of a family circle to surround him in his old age.

I had first come to know him through the director of the Islamic Museum, the tall, stately, erudite, and bearded Marwan Abu Khalaf, who, still in his thirties, directs the restoration of Arabic art objects on which Hassan and others like him work. The museum is located in the vast Haram al-Sharif "Sacred Place" that encompasses both the al-Aqsa Mosque, a basilica, and the Dome of the Rock, a cupola building.

One day, early in our friendship, Hassan and I visited the magnificent Dome of the Rock. We stepped onto a raised, terracelike platform that is surrounded by pillars with stairways on every side. The octagonal masterpiece is fashioned with blue and green tiles that shine in the Mediterranean light with fierce prismatic symmetry. I looked above to an incredibly large yet graceful dome of gold.

"Everyone nowadays, even the Muslims, refer to this as the Mosque of Omar, but Omar did not build it. Rather," Hassan related, "it was constructed by the order of Abdul-Malek Ibn Marwan, the Umayyah Caliph of Damascus. This was in 685."

At the entrance to the Dome of the Rock, Hassan and I, along with dozens of other visitors from around the world, removed our shoes and, once inside, walked on ancient, richly textured Oriental rugs. After a half-dozen steps we reached a guardrail that framed a large boulder. I was startled by the unexpected dimensions of the rock.

We stood silently. I saw a large mass of stone, mineral matter from the earth's crust, a boulder like other boulders I have seen in countless regions of the earth. The rock, which rises above the ground to my shoulders and covers an area half the size of a tennis court, dominates the entire space within the shrine. Visitors come here not specifically to pray, but to admire and revere the rock. This shrine—the most beautiful in Jerusalem and one of the most beautiful religious edifices in the world—was built for one sole purpose: to protect and enhance the huge rock.

If I saw mineral matter, old Hassan, looking at the rock, sees eternity. The rock, he believes, is the foundation stone of the universe. "It marks the center of the world," he told me. And the center of his faith. The holy stone, Hassan believes, antedates the three great religions, Judaism, Christianity, and Islam.

"Arabs called Amorites came here four or five thousand years ago. They established this site as a religious foundation to honor their god, who was called Shalem. And these early Arab worshipers of a God they called Shalem gave us the name of our Holy City, Jerusalem.

"Then Arabs from Canaan, who were called Canaanites, came here. They made Jerusalem an early center of worship of the One God. The Canaanites had a king named Melchizedek, and it is written that he also was priest of God Most High.

"All of this early Arab history predates the arrival of the Hebrews by many centuries. The point is that everyone in history has borrowed from what went before. There were countless battles over Jerusalem. And the Hebrews were in power here only sixty years.

"Muslims and Christians as well as Jews connect this great rock with Abraham," Hassan continued. "He began his journey to this rock in Mesopotamia between the Tigris and Euphrates rivers, a part of modern Iraq. He walked to what is now Turkey and later traveled to the Judean highlands of Jordan. Eventually, at this rock, he prepared, as a sign of his love of God, to sacrifice his son Isaac, but God stayed Abraham's hand.

"Muhammad tells us Abraham was the actual founder of our Islamic religion," Hassan continued. "Our quarrel has never been with Jews as Jews or with the great religion of Judaism. The places that the Jews and Christians revere as holy, we revere as holy. The prophets the Jews and Christians revere as holy, we revere as holy. My holy book the Koran is filled with devout references to Noah, Abraham, Moses, and Christ. As for this great rock," Hassan concluded, "Muhammad believed it had its origins in Paradise. And it was from this sacred rock that Muhammad was transported by God to heaven."

Before I had met Hassan, the force of Islam had hit me in a particular way—in the strength and intensity of one voice calling the faithful to prayer. I was living in a small Old City hostel and was not aware of the advent of Ramadan, the month-long Islamic religious observation. One morning before dawn I hear the voice of a crier from a nearby mosque, a voice that seems of unearthly volume. I do not understand the words, but I understand the command: Get up! Get up! And dress! And pray!

I make the bed. I dress. I wait, listening obediently. And in my submissiveness I am acting out the meaning of the word *Islam*.

The all-pervasive voice of the *muezzin*—raised through electronics to its highest decibel during Ramadan—demands that one take notice. From a terrace I watch about five thousand Muslims move inside the al-Aqsa mosque near the Dome of the Rock, and another five thousand gather in the mosque's vast courtyard to pray. Seeing the multitude, I feel a tiny droplet in a sea of Arabness that opens into a greater sea of Islam.

One noontime, soon after we met, I was in Hassan's office at the Islamic Museum. We heard the amplified recorded voice of a *muezzin* calling the faithful to prayers. "He gives orders for prayers to God, the God," Hassan explained. "He is telling us, God is nice for everybody. If you please, come for prayers." Hassan, like hundreds of millions of Muslims around the world, hears the *muezzin's* call to prayer five times a day: at dawn (or predawn), midday, midafternoon, sunset, and nightfall.

"I can pray anywhere—in my home, on the road, or at work," Hassan told me, and he pointed to a prayer rug neatly stored in a corner. Rolled out on the floor, it provides a clean place on which to pray.

Wherever he prays, he faces toward Mecca, kneels, bows down, and offers these words from the first chapter of the Koran, words that have been called by Christians "The Arabian Lord's Prayer":

> Praise be to God, the Lord of the worlds!
> The compassionate, the merciful!
> King on the day of reckoning!

Thee only do we worship, and to thee do
we cry for help.
Guide thou us on the straight path,
The path of those to whom thou has been
gracious: with whom
Thou art not angry, and who go not astray.

In addition to going to al-Aqsa Mosque on holy Friday, Hassan likes worshiping there on weekdays as well. "Praying in the mosque is not for a king or a prince only; it is for everybody. When the first line is full, somebody starts a second line. If the king is late, he fits in where he can."

I take his statement to mean that, by and large, it is average, every-day-of-the-week Islamic people who fill the mosques—people who are among the eight hundred million followers of Muhammad. After Christianity, Hassan's religion is the world's second religion. Every fifth person in the world is a Muslim. The Muslims live in forty nations, including Egypt, Turkey, Iraq, Iran, Afghanistan, Saudi Arabia, and Libya. And until 1948, and the creation of Israel within old Palestine, Islam was the dominant faith in what we call the Holy Land.

As a devout Muslim, Hassan obeys specific religious duties. "I do not eat pork nor drink anything alcoholic. During the month of Ramadan, I fast, not taking any food or water from dawn to sunset. I pray fives times a day. And I daily repeat the Creed: 'There is no god but God; and Muhammad is the Prophet of God.'"

One day I suggest to Hassan that I accompany him to pray in al-Aqsa Mosque. We leave his office, walk across a courtyard, and near the mosque, we stop at el Kas Fountain, used by Muslims for ritual washing before prayer. "This fountain, built by Arabs in 709, gets a continual flow of water from numerous underground cisterns near here," Hassan says. I stand and watch as Hassan sits on a circular concrete bench. He rolls his trousers to his knees and his shirt-sleeves above his elbows. Using an individual water tap, he washes his hands and arms to his elbows. Next, beginning with his toes, he washes his feet and his legs up to his knees. Cupping water in his hands, he washes his mouth, nose, ears, and neck. Then, standing, he rolls down his shirtsleeves and the legs of his trousers and announces, "Now I can pray. In front of God. I am clean."

Entering the mosque, I note the beauty of more than a hundred stained-glass windows fashioned in stylized, colorful arabesque designs. Here in this mosque, I recall, a crazed terrorist had shot and killed the grandfather of the present king of Jordan. And here in this mosque Egyptian President Anwar Sadat, while on his famous journey of peace, had knelt to pray. The Muslim judge called on Sadat to "listen to the voice of al-Aqsa, the voice of Palestine in mourning." And people shouted to Sadat as he left the mosque, "Remember Palestine, oh Sadat!"

Hassan and I remove our shoes, and again, as at the Dome of the Rock, we walk on luxurious handwoven carpets. While followers of Islam prefer no chairs but have carpets, Christians prefer no carpets but have chairs. Hassan makes a point of this difference, relating, "In 1099 after the Crusaders captured Muslim Jerusalem, the Christians promptly removed the carpets and installed chairs and made this mosque the headquarters of their Knights Templar. Then we won Jerusalem back, removed their chairs, and replaced our rugs."

Inside the mosque, Hassan and I separate. Traditionally in this land, male Muslims in their mosques, as well as male Jews in their synagogues, pray separately from women. Hassan joins hundreds of Muslim men who pray in the center and eastern sections. And I, moving to the western section of the mosque, join Arab women dressed in black. I stay quietly on my knees, watching the worshipers in long rows. When the leader, or *imam*, drops to his knees, placing his hands on the ground in front of him, and lowering his forehead in prostration, the worshipers make the same motions in the same moment. Then the *imam* stands and the worshipers stand. They accompany their movements with recitations from the Koran of adorations and praises of God. After prayers, the *imam* preaches a sermon dealing with the meaning of Islam.

Leaving the mosque, Hassan and I replace our shoes and once again we are in the vast Haram al-Sharif "Sacred Place," a rectangular area larger than thirty football fields. This religious area, the largest in the Holy Land, represents about one-twentieth of the Old City. Who, I ask Hassan, manages all this area?

"We have a Supreme Muslim Council that administers all Muslim property and Muslim affairs," he replies. "Then the council has an executive arm called the *waqf*, which controls this area as well as thirty-five other mosques, many cemeteries, and other Islamic religious sites within the Old City. This Old Walled City throughout its long history has been predominantly inhabited by Arabs. And today Arab markets, Arab homes, and Arab religious sites make up about ninety percent of the Old City.

"You will not find any important Jewish monuments or religious sanctuaries in Jerusalem," Hassan adds, reminding me that "the Jews left here two thousand years ago."

We descended a series of steps from the raised Haram al-Sharif area and saw Jews praying at what is called the Western or Wailing Wall. "That wall actually is Muslim property," Hassan continues. "The Jews claim that the wall is a remnant of Solomon's Temple, but it is in fact part of the outer wall of Herod's Temple. It is historically established that Solomon's Temple was completely demolished more than once. Many archaeologists have dug here, and they have not come up with any remnants of Solomon's Temple."

Nevertheless, the tradition holds that Solomon's Temple sat on the summit of this Holy Mount, and after it was destroyed the Jews came to the Western Wall of Herod's Temple to bewail its destruction. The site became known as the Wailing Wall, and it is the only old site where the Jews pray in Jerusalem.

The Old City of Jerusalem is one of the few remaining examples in the world of a completely walled town. The walls stand partially on the foundations of Hadrian's Square, built in A.D. 135. They include remains of earlier walls, those of King Herod in 37 B.C., and Agrippa, A.D. 41, and Saladin, 1187. And finally the walls were rebuilt by the Turkish Muslim, Suleiman the Magnificent, in the sixteenth century.

"An indigenous people, a people who never left Palestine, continually have lived within these old walls," Hassan relates. "I can trace my forebears back more than ten generations. We have always lived within the Old City and for three hundred years in the same house." He fears that the Old City is being obliterated by Israelis who confiscate Arab land and build skyscrapers, encircling Old Jerusalem.

"The Old City goes back to the days of Christ, whereas West Jerusalem is less than one hundred years old. And most of it was built in the past three decades. The newcomers who build the skyscrapers are not a Semitic people but rather Westerners from Europe and America who have no appreciation for our holy sites."

He and I, walking within the Old City, pause at Damascus Gate, which, he says, typifies the Old City. Suleiman the Magnificent built it in 1537 as the main entrance to his fortress. Hassan points out that the old gate, being no taller than a four-story building, is not grandiose as measured by the skyscrapers encircling Jerusalem. Yet with its solid wings, turrets, and massive tower, it projects strength, beauty, and endurance. "It is far more beautiful than any new building in New Jerusalem."

From Damascus Gate it is an easy walk to Jaffa Gate in the west. "Arabs call this gate 'the Gate of Khalil,' a word meaning friend. It is our name for Abraham," Hassan explains. He points to an Arabic inscription over the gate: "There is no god but God, and Abraham is the friend of God." Dignitaries who in modern times have entered Jaffa Gate with flags flying and bands playing include the first English bishop in 1841, the German Kaiser in 1898, and British Field Marshal Edmund Allenby in 1917. After Allenby made his triumphant entry, "I was no longer a subject of the Turks," Hassan recalls. "I and all the Palestinians became British subjects."

Besides Damascus and Jaffa, there is the Dung Gate in the south and St. Stephen's Gate in the east. And there are Zion and Herod's gates. Also there is an eighth gate called the Golden Gate that is now walled up.

Hassan, like all fundamentalists who accept a literal, word-for-word interpretation of Holy Scripture, believes that on Judgment Day the Golden Gate will be opened. The saved souls now buried throughout the world will rise from their graves. If they have not been buried in Jerusalem, they will get to the Holy City and position themselves to walk through this Golden Gate to Paradise.

The Golden Gate and, for that matter, all the gates leading into the Old City are so small they would not, as presently constructed, accommodate the traffic flowing across the Brooklyn Bridge. Everything about the Old City is small and compressed and like a miniature world, and of course that is its marvel and its miracle. It is a world set in a frame. It can and does represent all humankind and our concept of one God.

The Old City, in short, is manageable, for our minds and for our legs. One can easily walk the circumference of the ramparts, a distance of two and a half miles. And given a little time, one can memorize the zigzagging, labyrinthine twists and turns of the Old City corridors that on one's first meanderings seem a formidable maze.

Within the Old City, Hassan and I walk in a network of narrow alleys closely woven into the texture of the buildings. We are in an old vaulted suk—the colonnades giving shelter from the sun and rain—that has been the main market of Jerusalem for two thousand years. Vendors and buyers and pilgrims and the frankly curious are up close, and colors and sounds and smells seem intensified. Everyone is swept along; everyone is able to touch.

Moving in the crowded alleyways, we rub shoulders with an Arab whose head is swathed in a kerchief called a keffiya. We see another Arab whose head is crowned with a Turkish-style fez. We pass Franciscans in their brown habits, Greek Orthodox priests in black, a Muslim religious teacher, called a mullah, in a silk gown and carrying a gold-topped cane, and orthodox Hasidic Jews who, despite the searing summer heat, wear the long black frock coats and wide fur hats that they or their forebears wore in the cold clime of Poland.

We see devout American Christians, retracing the steps of Christ with his Cross, prayer books in hand. Next to the pilgrims, an Arab with a polished brass tea urn strapped to his back and glasses fitted like cartridges around his waist dispenses a glass of hot tea to a standing customer, while a barefoot Arab youth zigzags four sheep around us all.

I am jostled by a Roman Catholic priest, the next minute by booted, khaki-uniformed Israeli soldiers weighted with tear-gas canisters, ammunition belts, walkie-talkies, Uzi rifles, and submachine guns. They maneuver around an old Arab bent double with crates of poultry, and another Arab with a goat carcass slung like a cape around his neck. We brush against laughing, pinafored Arab schoolgirls, an old, blind beggar and a handsome young Arab policeman named Mousa with dark eyes and sardonic smile. We pass Arab women dressed in black with their faces veiled, yet moving with radarlike precision.

The suk is unique not only because of its antiquity and the variety of its wares, but also because Jerusalem is a crossroads for the East and West. Like any open public market in the Orient, this suk assaults my senses. I step around an open sewer and smell excrement, then take another step and inhale the most delicious aroma of honey cake. Nothing is neatly separated, nothing has been put into cellophane. All seems like raw nerve ends, and as real as this fleeting moment. It seems a contradiction that the holiest shrines of three faiths should be tucked away amid the stalls where vendors hawk honey cakes, leather goods, pots and pans, hardware, eggplants and garlic, fish, and slabs of meat from carcasses of goats.

Elsewhere, one seems to find holy sites in more appropriate settings. I recall a visit to the Big Buddha statue in Japan and a visit to Mont-Saint-Michel on the pinnacle of a steep rock in Normandy, France, and in each instance the surroundings and my approach gave me an opportunity to ponder the meaning of the Buddha and the meaning of the island monastery. I have also visited other great and marvelous sites, not necessarily religious, but inspiring. I think of the Taj Mahal in India, the Pyramids in Egypt, and Machu Picchu in Peru, and my approach to each permitted me to concentrate on what I would soon see. But here, millions of pilgrims travel to Jerusalem, and they find that the most holy ground is set in an Arab bazaar.

Also, of course, it is a hometown for Arabs such as Hassan, who was born here, who bought his first pair of shoes here, got his first shave from a barber in the Old City, was fitted for his first suit of clothes in the Old City, was married here, saw all his children born here, watched them grow up here. And he will die here.

Hassan points above the milling mob to show me how many of the old houses lean on and overlap one another. He explains that most tourists, intently observing the wares and bizarre sights of the *suk*, do not see the homes that are tucked out of sight.

One home along the alleyway is different, however. Hassan points above the door to blue Arabic script that proclaims that the owner of this home and his wife have made the pilgrimage called *hadj* to the holy Islamic city of Mecca. The owner of this house is Hassan himself, and he is prouder of having made *hadj* than of any other accomplishment in his life. In the Old City and throughout the Islamic world, a show of piety commands respect, and nothing commands more respect than a Muslim who displays evidence of a pilgrimage to Mecca.

Hassan unlocks the door and leads me up the steps. We reach a second level, walk across a small courtyard, pass under a clothesline, and enter a kitchen. Here Hassan introduces me to a daughter-in-law who is married to his son, Khalid, who teaches Arab students in a school run by the Israelis.

From the kitchen, Hassan and I walk across marble floors inlaid with patterned, brillantly hued stones into the living quarters. We sit on a velvet sofa, and his daughter-in-law brings Dresden cups with minted tea and a hand-wrought silver bowl filled with fruit. I look to a high ceiling with wooden beams carved and painted in royal blue and inlaid with gold. These are small remnants of a once great and glorious past when Arab forebears ruled half the known world and were the favored of God.

"My grandfather Hassan, who worked for the ministry of foreign affairs during the time of the Ottoman Empire, lived here. Later he resigned from the government and became a merchant," Hassan relates. He was expected to carry on in the steps of his grandfather and father and become a merchant, but he chose to study art. For many years he studied sculpture and painting under Italian artists living in Jerusalem.

"After the British gained control over Jerusalem, the English authorities named me inspector of all government buildings in Jerusalem, as well as one of the supervisors of the Palestine Museum," now called the Rockefeller Museum, in East Jerusalem. Earlier, he and I had visited this museum and Hassan had explained that he was with the team that excavated at the caves at Qumran and recovered fragments of the oldest known biblical manuscripts, the Dead Sea Scrolls. On the day he and I had visited the museum he proudly showed me forty-eight jars he had restored from excavation fragments. For years, during the British mandate, he personally held the key to the museum and was responsible for closing and opening it each day. "The British knew me to be an honest man," he said.

Hassan has five sons who were working outside East Jerusalem at the time the Israelis militarily occupied this territory. Now, he said, "the Israelis will not permit my sons to return home, not even for a visit." They include Tisizer in Libya, Zakiah in Saudia Arabia, Inam in Kuwait, and Ali and Fias who work in Jordan.

Hassan and his wife wanted to visit their sons, Ali and Fias, in Jordan, and asked permission to go there. Palestinians living in the

West Bank and Gaza have no passport and therefore must request Israeli permission any time they wish to travel outside their homeland, such as for a visit to relatives in Jordan. Israeli authorities denied Hassan the right to travel but granted his wife a permit.

I saw her after she returned from the border crossing, which is heavily guarded by soldiers, and she said that as much as she loved her sons she would not make the trip again. "The Israeli soldiers searched not only all of my possessions, but they forced me to undress and they inspected my private parts." She told me this "in secret," saying that she would never tell her husband. As for Hassan, he said he was glad his wife could see their sons, but that the Israelis giving her a permit to go to Jordan was no substitute for permitting the return of his sons. He pointed out that Israel's refusal to permit the return of displaced Palestinians violates the Fourth Geneva convention, which protects persons temporarily absent from an occupied area.

"I am Palestinian; my sons are Palestinians. We were born here; my families have lived here for at least ten generations. I want my children to come home," Hassan said, his voice strained and tired. "I wrote to the Israeli authorities at least a hundred times, asking that my children be permitted to return home. We are not from Poland or Russia or Albania. We are from here. 'I am sorry,' the Israelis answer. 'No permission for your children.'

"Who are the ones who refuse the Palestinians the right to return home? Strangers with blue eyes and blond hair. They may become citizens in my homeland. I do not have a hatred for blue eyes as such—many Muslims have blue eyes and light hair—but I hate the fact that the Israeli government welcomes any Jew from any part of the world to live as a citizen in a country where my children were born but now are not permitted to live."

Hassan often reminded me that the United States supports Israel in its wartime measures, such as arbitrary separation of Palestinian families. For a while, he saw me as an individual and accepted me as an individual, but when he saw me talking to the young fair-haired South African Jew outside the museum, Hassan no doubt thought with irony and bitterness that this young Jew had come from another land and been welcomed and provided a home, while his own sons could not return to the land where they were born. He saw the young Jew, and even me, I now believe, as one of "them" who separated him from his greatest dream and his agonized, overwhelming desire: to be reunited with his sons.

"I fear I will die without ever being reunited with my children," he once told me. "There are thousands of Palestinian parents like me. Our bitterness against the occupation is growing."

Kamil,
a Muslim Merchant

Now I have lived through Ramadan. The month-long period when Muslims fast during the daylight hours is officially ended. I see young Arab boys riding donkeys in the streets, shouting in celebration. Old Arab women and men put on their best clothes. And I hear the explosion of fireworks. Yet a Roman Catholic nun who had lived in other Islamic countries tells me, "The Arabs here are subdued. The gun is over them." She then adds, ominously. "But the anger against the occupation forces is deep—and growing."

On another occasion, I hear a European visitor tell this same nun, "I will come back in two years to the Holy Land," and the nun adds, "If there is a Holy Land."

Throughout history—a turbulent three-thousand-year history when it has been besieged, burned, sacked, and repeatedly rebuilt—Jerusalem has been a beacon of the spirit, yet always a center of strife. The tension and the strife remain. And the tension enters into me and, like a recurring malady, saps my strength.

Then, walking around the old walls, I might touch the stones. Nothing special you might say, limestone, or what is called Jerusalem limestone, and I study the veins of the old stones as one might read the palms of a hand and try to decipher what is written, what is the future.

Always the stones remind me that the business of Jerusalem is eternity. Not for this race or this creed. But at least for these stones. Tough yet noble, they vary in shades from a yellowish-gray through pink-gold to russet-gold. In the old walls the stones dating from the Roman days and Suleiman the Magnificent have weathered to become yellower than most, and there are some hours in the afternoon when they shine like slabs of gold. I see the walls, towers, spires, and pinnacles that represent the three faiths. Yet, although the Old City is a holy city to three faiths, I look upon a scene that is predominantly Muslim Arab.

Everyday, I walk the dirt and cobblestoned streets of Old Jerusalem. I see certain vendors, and eventually come to know a Greek, Demetri, about thirty-five and very handsome. I have stopped so often in his souvenir shop that he wonders if I want him for an adventure. He takes me aside and explains his plight: he wants to do what he can ... but conditions are so crowded in his shop, and he lives in the nearby St. John Monastery. I say I understand, that I am independent and not lonely. We become talking friends.

Demetri, I casually ask, how long has your family been in Jerusalem?

"I was born here in the Old City. And my father before me. And his father. We have lived four hundred years here in Jerusalem," he replies.

Demetri sells a wide variety of souvenirs, including the Crusader cross, the Maltese cross, the Star of David, seven-branched candelabra, copper from Acre, brass from Nazareth, mother-of-pearl-encrusted boxes from Bethlehem, and olive wood from Gethsemane.

How, I ask, does one become a merchant in the *suk*? "You buy a key," he tells me, adding that the key to his shop now is valued at eighty thousand dollars.

Who owns the Old City? I ask Demetri. He reaffirms what Hassan had said: that about ninety percent of the Old City shops are run by Muslims. "But the property itself is owned by the Greek Orthodox Christians, the Supreme Muslim Council, the Roman Catholics, and private business. And a few of the stores are owned by Armenians and Christian Arabs."

Leaving Demetri I walk to the Church of the Holy Sepulcher, and in its recesses I find a cubbyhole where a photographer, Zaki Zaarour, has a small office. An Arab Muslim who photographs Christian pilgrims and sells them the prints, Zaki welcomes me graciously and asks, "Do you want coffee?" A six-year-old Arab child materializes with a swinging tray that holds a small cup of strong, thick, aromatic Arabic coffee.

"I have a brother who drives a cab in Washington, D.C.," Zaki relates. "He married an American. My brother was accustomed to working eighteen hours in this country and, after he got to America—and he waited years to get there—he proceeded to work even harder for his future and his security—but his American wife wanted to go out evenings. Now they are divorced and he is unhappy. He still loves her," Zaki says.

Later, I pass a vendor who works in a souvenir shop near the Holy Selpulcher. I see him regularly and learn that his name is Ali. He is about fifty, short and thin and balding, with high cheekbones and olive-toned skin. In the late evenings, when I am returning home, I often see Ali at the Central Cafe, near the Jaffa Gate. Once, hot and exhausted after a day's travel, I responded to the owner's "Welcome, Welcome," and walked inside and ordered a glass of freshly squeezed grapefruit juice.

Ali, seated nearby, was smoking a water pipe called a *narghile*. I ask if he is smoking hashish. "No, pure tobacco," he says. Almost immediately, Ali begins to talk to me of sex, and the need of a man for a woman, a woman for a man. Ali, by living in the Old City, lives in olden times. The Old City has no football or baseball teams to cheer, no bowling. No theater, opera, concerts, movies. Conversation with a man like Ali is necessarily limited. He wants to know about my ethnic background. "What is your blood?" he asks.

What difference does it make, I reply, what religion my father was, what religion my mother was? What skin color he had, and she had? All blood, I insist, is red blood.

But he wants to know if I'm Jewish? Or Christian? In this part of the world, everyone wants and maybe even needs to know, and once this is known, then the conversation will go in a certain way.

On another day I see Mousa, an Arab Muslim policeman. I came to know Mousa by having been thrust against him in the ongoing traffic of the *suk*. In the inadvertent eyeball-to-eyeball encounter, I saw dark and handsome features, and my eyes lingered. Now Mousa invites me to a small outdoor cafe for a Turkish coffee.

"Do you know how long I have worked?" he asks. "I am twenty-nine and was born of a poor family, and I have worked for eighteen years, having earned my own living since I was eleven." He has beautiful skin and eyes. But unlike many Arabs who speak with resonance and a deepness of tone, his voice is high pitched and strained.

Two Jewish girls in tight bust-and-derriere-revealing khaki uniforms pass by.

Do Arab men date Jewish girls? I ask Mousa.

"Yes. But never marry them. In Israel, only a Jew can marry another Jew. My religion permits me to marry a non-Muslim. The woman may agree to become Muslim but she doesn't have to."

Once, as Mousa and I are walking through the Old City, we pass a small fruit-and-vegetable stand operated by a man I know to be fair with his prices, and I wave to him—I know him as Kamil. As we walk on, Mousa, who keeps his own FBI-type file on all the inhabitants in the Old City, relates that some years ago Kamil had discovered a younger brother making love with another man and "he shot his brother." Kamil had been sentenced to prison and had escaped after about twelve years.

Kamil was about fifty, pencil-thin, almost completely bald, and with two front teeth missing. As a child I had heard the expression that it was easy to love God because God had first loved me. This also applied to my friendship with Kamil, for I found it easy to accept a friendship that had been initiated by him when he gave me fair prices when I first stopped at his stand for apples and bananas. On my next visit, a week or so later—and Kamil would have watched a stream of tens of thousands of tourists and shoppers in the interim, for this was one of the busiest markets in the world—Kamil had expressed a surprised joy in seeing me again. I told him I remembered his prices because they were fair.

"The people like me because I am honest with them. Honest is better. If I am not honest, I am not at rest with myself," he says. He moves a crate and I enter the booth and sit on a wooden box while he walks to a nearby shop to order tea. Kamil returns, and soon a young Arab boy appears with the tea. I know that the vendors have little or no hot water to scald dishes, and that I will be drinking out of a cup shared by hundreds of others.

In the intimacy of his small shop Kamil talks in a poetic or singsong manner. "It is nice the day I see you. Very nice."

Kamil was happy on the days when I sat in the back of his stall, and I felt happy too. I felt a kind of comfort or security there because until I had met him I had been on the outside looking into these booths, and he allowed me to come inside, to see it all from the vantage point of the one who lives there.

A Greek woman stops and bargains in Greek for garlic. When she leaves, laden with kilos of garlic, I ask Kamil where he had learned his Greek.

"I learned it the same way I learned Hebrew, English, German, and Italian—in this booth, talking with people." He adds that the Arab merchants in the Old City have to be "very clever" and "know many languages" to pay the rent on their market stalls. In his facility for languages, Kamil was typical of other Arab merchants. I heard them speaking German to Germans, Hebrew to Jews, Italian to Italians—and I did not meet one Arab in the Old City who was not fluent in English.

Kamil liked talking with me about his work, spreading out his life for me to review. He went in predawn hours each morning to a central Arab market to buy the produce he carried to his booth, which he opened at 7:00 A.M., and closed about 7:00 P.M., although I frequently saw him there even later. When I reminded him once that he had been standing twelve hours, he shrugged his shoulders. "Working, I feel strong," he bragged. Here he seemed typically male, revealing his happiness standing before a woman who would listen—and I watched him attempt to square his thin, stooped shoulders as he insisted he could work twenty-four hours, "and without food."

He cared little for food, although he drank coffee or tea when I joined him. And at the back of the shop he kept an opened box of cheap, stale cookies on which he munched, never stopping for a regular breakfast or lunch.

Kamil had six children, and he talked with me about the rising cost of books. Each day they were told to bring a little money for this kind of purchase or these kinds of taxes, and Kamil said he did not know how he could continue to meet the demands that were made on him. He talked of inflation as the ever-present monster that ate away his life.

Yet, often as I sat talking with him, customers would inspect his fruits or vegetables, and Kamil would ignore them, or if they asked for his attention he might respond indifferently. He gave no sales pitch and never haggled over prices. I suggested he was not giving the customers enough attention.

He smiled indulgently and eventually in the singsong way of expressing himself let me know that he had long ago learned his trade.

"The one who wants to buy, I know him. The man who does not want to buy, I know him. I am like a doctor who feels the pulse."

With Kamil I came to realize that I have two kinds of friends, some such as Hassan, whom I can disappoint and thereby lose, and others such as my mother and Kamil, whom I can treat with impunity, since each seems to feel that whatever I do I mean well. Often when I left his booth he would extract a promise that I would return, say on a Wednesday or a Monday, or that I would meet him at Damascus Gate on a certain Friday, his free day, when he wanted to show me "the Holy sites." That day would come and I would be busy or not so inclined. And I would fail to keep the appointment.

I could not telephone, so I went on my way and hoped that he read my mind, and then I put him out of my mind. Days or weeks would pass, and I would suddenly feel the need of the warmth of his hospitality. It seems some of us need those who never place a demand on you, and, since he never did, he became a kind of ballast in my life—and so I would stride through the old corridors toward his stall. And along the way I might wonder what kind of excuse will I give, and as quickly as the thought came I dismissed it, for I knew I did not need to play a talking game with him. He would not ask, I need not explain, he would invite me for a tea or a coffee, and insist that I sit in his booth, and he would rejoice in the moment that we shared. And that was in fact the way it always happened.

One day after an absence of some weeks, I again go for a visit. Seeing me, his eyes behind his thick glasses light up, and his mouth, with his front teeth missing, opens in a smile. In his British accent he asks where had I been, and that is followed quickly by his usual, "Tea or coffee?" Knowing that neither was inexpensive and that he had a big family and little money, I declined, insisting I was not thirsty, but he seemed not to hear. Ordering the drinks was as much a part of his ritual as his removing a case of eggplants or onions to clear a path for me to enter his stall.

Earlier I had come to know two Arab men, and each had invited me into his home. Their wives had cooked for me, and I had met their children—one man had eight, the other had fourteen, the youngest one month old. In each instance, since the families were by my Western monetary standards extremely poor, I left bills where the woman of the house would find them. Several days later when, on different occasions, I saw each of the men in the Old City, neither was happy to see me. Each treated me like a stranger, and each said

I should not have left the money. I told all this to Kamil, stressing one point: the men had so little. And he said what I should have known: "Yes, about all they have is their pride, and you took that."

On this day a young man, who appears almost twice the height and weight of Kamil, comes to the booth. He has blondish hair and rather handsome features, and I cannot think of him as the son of Kamil, but that is the way Kamil presents him. I learn his name is Fawzi, and when I ask his age, which I guess to be seventeen or eighteen, he replies with a grin, "No, maybe twenty or twenty-two," leaving me as uncertain as before I asked.

"I want to get married," he tells me. He is the opposite of his father, who carefully edits himself before he speaks and speaks so frugally I can readily recall all he ever said.

If he gets married, I suggest, he will need money. Does he work? Yes, he says, *inside*, for the Jews.

Fawzi and, I suppose, other Arabs like him, think of Arabs as living in the big, *outside* world, and the Jews living in an exclusive or "inside" world composed only of other Jews.

Kamil and I are toward the back of the small stall, and Fawzi is up front, weighing the produce that the customers want, a bag of carrots or a cauliflower.

I repeat to the father what the son has told me: that he works for the Jews.

"One day he is working; one week he is sleeping," Kamil says. He adds that the boy knows that "I am working and I will be feeding him. He sleeps at home, laughs, eats—and leaves." Kamil concludes, "All the young people are the same. They hate the work."

Fawzi, having completed a sale, repeats in a casual, flippant tone that he wants to marry. "I want to marry an American," and he hesitates as if he has dreamed too wildly, and amends that to say, "Or an Arab Jewish woman." He works in a small Israeli factory where, he says, many young Sephardic Jewish girls work, and he likes them. "Arab Jewish, very nice," he says.

It is not at all unusual for an Arab such as Fawzi to be attracted to Jewish women, nor for that matter for Jewish men to be attracted to Arab women. In Fawzi's case, however, he sees a Jewish woman as being a step upward.

Many Arab youths told me that under the Israeli occupation they saw their fathers as vulnerable, helpless, second class, even inferior, and because they felt themselves to be brainwashed into accepting that one group—the Jews—was higher or somehow better than the other, they found it difficult not to hate themselves. Fawzi impresses me as one who wants to leave the inferior world of his father. In fact, he told me he hates the Old City. He yearns to align himself with a Jewish woman, and he says Arab Jewish because they, speaking the Arabic language, eating Arabic food, and enjoying Arabic music, are accessible to him. But eventually he dreams that ultimate dream, to align himself with an American woman.

With Fawzi up front, out of our conversational range, I comment to Kamil that the boy thinks he can go to the United States and find it easy, as easy as heaven.

"He can find work anywhere," Kamil responds. "He can get a girl anywhere. If he uses his brain, he will be in heaven; if he does not use his brain, he will not be in heaven—regardless of where he is. God gave us a brain; it is our greatest treasure." Then, speaking of Fawzi's addiction to peer pressures, he adds, "I must treat him as a small boy. His mind now is crazy." He repeats what he told me earlier, "All the young people are the same."

After leaving Kamil that day I wondered if patience and psychology had come to him by self-examination during his long years in prison. He saw the role of a shopkeeper somewhat equivalent to that of a psychiatrist. He did not use that word, but he said that he treated his customers as he did his son: "One must be quiet; one must be kind to people. Always treat them kindly."

Once, taking a chance that he wanted me to know about his past, I asked Kamil outright, had he shot his brother? His face registered great surprise, and then relief. He then knew that his past was not important to me, and I felt this made us closer friends.

With Palestinians
in Jerusalem

"Here," said an acquaintance named Mouhib, pointing near an intersection where we stood, "here is where—to create a state for European Jews out of a land that had been Arab for thousands of years—they ran a knife through Palestine and through Jerusalem, and gave that part" and he motions to the west "to the Jews, leaving this part to the east, along with the Old Walled City, to the Arabs."

He and I stand on ground left to the Arabs, in what today is called Arab East Jerusalem. We are about three blocks from Damascus Gate and the Old Walled City, at the intersection of Nablus and Nebi Samuel roads. Looking across the intersection, I see the East Jerusalem American Consulate Office, where Mouhib, an Arab Muslim, works as translator and clerk.

As I would learn, Mouhib and his family, and especially his father, al-Hammuri, who lost most of his property at the time Israel was created, have lived a history that today affects all our lives.

The man who stands at my side is now forty-two, a college graduate, with dark eyes and dark hair. Unlike so many Arabs who are tall and slender, Mouhib is built solidly, with facial features as well as a body indicating strength. This man, the youngest of eight children, is taking me back to the time he was a child and lived "in a big house" in what is now called West Jerusalem.

"I was ten years old when the state of Israel was created. In that year, 1948, my brother Asad crossed from West Jerusalem through the so-called Mandelbaum gate. There was no such gate, but only a narrow passage. He went into Jordan. Until this day," Mouhib adds, "Asad has never been permitted to return. He was twenty-two when he left, and now he is fifty-four and still living in Amman, still hoping one day to return home and see our father."

Mouhib speaks often of his father, who, since the death of his wife, lives with Mouhib and his wife and children. One Sunday Mouhib invites me to his home for lunch, and I meet his father, his wife, who is named Rasmiya, and their children. Rasmiya, slender and attractive, enacts her typical feminine role by remaining most of the time in the kitchen with their two eldest daughters. While they prepare lunch Mouhib takes his youngest children to a relative's home for a birthday party. I am left with his father, al-Hammuri, seventy-five, a large, rotund man, who was educated in Cambridge, England. His second son, he tells me, recently was killed in an automobile accident and, on hearing the news, "I lost most of my sight. The news killed a big part of me."

Like many aging persons who are unhappy about the present, the father turns his thoughts to the past. He speaks of Aristotle, Plato, Pythagoras, Euclid, Hippocrates, and Galen as if they were next-door neighbors. He says that nowadays all great Western thinkers regard the Greeks the way he does, but the Greeks were unknown to the West for centuries, and it was the Arabs, al-Hammuri reminds me, who discovered the legacy of their great civilization and gave it to the West. He suggests that this Arab discovery and the transportation of the greatest of thought to the Western world were infinitely more important than the transportation to the West of silks and spices from China or gold and silver from Peru.

As an example, he mentions a Spanish Arab philosopher named Averroes. Students of philosophy in Paris, Padua, and Bologna all studied his interpretive material "and through Averroes came to their first understanding of Aristotle.

"Arab mathematicians developed most branches of trigonometry and astronomy. And they gave us algebra. Europe learned Arabic numerals from an Arab named Khwarizmi. He taught the science of algebra and the most valid astronomical tables of his age.

Another Arab, al-Biruni, who laid the foundations for modern astronomy, was "one of the very greatest scientists of all time. He gave an accurate determination of latitude and longitude. He investigated the relative speeds of sound and light. And six hundred years before Galileo he discussed the possibility of the earth's rotation round its own axis."

Al-Hammuri mentions another Arab who lived in the sixteenth

century and became known as Leo Africanus, "the greatest geographer of Africa."

In studying the early great Arab thinkers, "I was always struck by the broad-mindedness they manifested," Al-Hammuri concludes. "In the Greek tradition, they taught that there can be no exclusivity in our quest for truth. They showed us that science, instead of being a denial of faith, can be its affirmation."

As we sit talking, Mouhib's wife serves us small glasses of *arrack*, made from grapes but stronger than wine. Al-Hammuri sips his drink—"I am Muslim but not one who believes God wants us to be dour"—and shows me diaries he has kept of history as he has seen it transpire.

"In 1905, when I was born, Palestine was under the Ottoman Empire. There were about fifty thousand Jews in Palestine. They were Sephardic, or Arab, Jews. There were so few German or Ashkenazic Jews they could not muster a quorum for a synagogue. The Arab Jews then in Jerusalem were of a Palestinian strain. We got along well. We did business together. We spoke a common language. In early Arabic literature you will find many testimonies of good relations between the Jews and the Arabs. The Muslims ruled over a large portion of the known world for thirteen hundred years, from the rise of Islam to the beginning of this century, and in this time the Muslims did not hate the Jews nor practice discrimination. We were brother-people and lived together in peace.

"Muslims venerated the great Jewish philosopher and physician Moses Maimonides, and the Muslim ruler Saladin chose him as his closest adviser and friend, as well as his personal physician.

"We Palestinian Arabs made no objections to the early arrival of European Jews in Palestine and the peaceful settlements made through the financial aid of Moses Montefiore and, in the eighteeneighties, by the Rothschilds. We did not see these Jews as threats to our lives and our properties. Arabs and Jews continued to live in peace. Our quarrel was never with Jews as Jews but with Jews as militant Zionists.

"The Zionists held their first international congress in Basel, Switzerland, in 1897," he continues. "These Zionists were not religious, but nationalistic. They were white European colonists who believed they were superior to people of color, to Orientals in particular. They had one goal: to take all of Palestine. To force out the Arabs. Never mind what we must suffer.

"The Zionists applied political pressure in England, which was at war with both Germany and Turkey, and in 1917 the English issued the Balfour Declaration, which favored the establishment of a 'Jewish national home in Palestine.'

"Soon afterward, the First World War ended. I saw a victorious British General Allenby enter Jerusalem, and I was present for the swearing in of the British High Commissioner. The Ottoman Rule was ended. But Palestine remained about ninety percent Palestinian Arab.

"The Jewish Agency became an official Jewish governing body within the British mandatory government, empowered to facilitate the immigration and settlement of Jews on Arab land.

"We thought it absurd for Europeans to speak of a 'return' to Palestine of white European Jews. They were not Orientals. They had no Palestinian strains. They had never lived in Palestine. Yet we were forced to relinquish our land to an alien race. Millions of dollars raised in the United States, South Africa, and England subsidized the European Jews who moved onto our best, most fertile Western or coastal plains.

"Then the Zionists began a series of attacks against the British and stepped up their violence and terrorism. Today their leaders call Palestinian Arabs who fight for freedom 'terrorists,' yet they are proud of their roles as 'terrorists.'

"Menachem Begin was well known as a leader of a terrorist gang. He wrote a book in which he boasts of his terrorism, including the wholesale massacre of innocent women and children. We find it ironic that the West honored him with a Nobel Peace Prize. Here is a man who readily admits being responsible for the 1948 massacre of two hundred fifty men, women, and children in the Arab village of Deir Yassin. Begin was head of the Irgun terrorist gang at the time. The massacre was carried out by members of both the Irgun and Stern gangs and helped trigger the flight of a million Arabs from the territories of what is now the state of Israel.

"The Jewish terrorists increased their pressure against the British—including blowing up a wing of the King David Hotel and killing ninety-one persons. And eventually the British left Palestine.

"And then Israel was declared a state. This was in 1948. In this year the Palestinian Arabs were still the majority, with about two-thirds of the population. Creating Israel meant giving the Jewish third of the population control over half the country that was ninety-percent owned by the Palestinian two-thirds of the population. Having won•this state, the Israelis seized my property in what is now West Jerusalem. We lived next to a home that for many years we had rented to Jews. We were the closest of friends. They came in tears and said, 'We would like to continue paying you rent.' That was not permitted. All my property was taken. Now I pass the home that was my home, and I am not allowed to go inside."

Mouhib returns with his children, and we all sit down to lunch. As we eat, al-Hammuri attempts to capsule the rest of his history.

"After the 1967 war, the Israelis tore down the stone walls between Arab Jerusalem and Jewish Jerusalem, and illegally annexed Arab East Jerusalem. We were one hundred thousand Arabs living in East Jerusalem—many of us, like my family, driven here after our lands were confiscated in West Jerusalem—and we had our mayor and our municipality. Our Arab municipal council previously had rejected Israel's proposal to join their municipality. We also protested the idea of annexation to the United Nations. The Israelis evicted two hundred Arab families from the Old City and moved in European Jews. I met with twenty Muslim leaders in al-Aqsa mosque and we issued a manifesto denouncing the annexation. As a response Israeli soldiers put four of our leaders under house arrest.

"The Israelis began deporting anyone who dared object to their taking our homes. They deported the president of the Islamic Court of Appeals. Shaykh Abd al-Hamid al-Sayih was the first person deported by Israel. Then they deported our Jerusalem mayor, Rouhi Khatib, as well as many of my friends who were well-respected doctors, judges, and bank managers. All the while they were arresting and deporting our leaders, they told the world their illegal annexation was a 'unification.' What kind of unification is it to expropriate our lands and buildings? I watched as they expropriated eight hundred acres of our best land in East Jerusalem. They bulldozed Arab homes to put in their Jewish settlements.

"We sit by helpless. We watch the Jews move into the Arab communities of Shufat, Beit Hanina, Bethlehem, and Beit Jala. They want to drive us all out. In 1948, they were given half of Jerusalem and half of Palestine. And now they want the other half as well. It seems there is no limit to the power of the usurper and his capacity to find justification for seizing Arab property, the rule being, 'What is mine is mine and what is yours is also mine.'"

After our lunch, Mouhib flips on the radio for the latest news. Israel announces it will take over the East Jerusalem Electric Company, for which al-Hammuri, until his recent retirement, had worked.

"The company provides electricity to East Jerusalem and a large area of the West Bank," he explains, adding that it has long been a symbol that East Jerusalem is not a part of Israel. Now, hearing of the projected take-over, he sighs:

"They leave us nothing. They took control of our roads, telephones, water, and other services. And now they want our East Jerusalem Electric Company."

Several weeks pass. I go by the American Consulate and invite Mouhib for lunch. We walk to a nearby cafe and sit American-style on tall stools before a counter. After lunch we stroll along Saladin, one of the main streets in East Jerusalem, and Mouhib greets a large, genial merchant, standing, as is often the Arab custom, outside his shop. In introducing me Mouhib says a name that sounds familiar, the name of Terzi.

Is he related, I ask, to Zehdi Terzi, the Palestine Liberation Organization observer to the United Nations General Assembly?

"Yes," the Jerusalem merchant tells me proudly, "we are brothers." His brother, a white-haired, bearded man who in newspaper photos seems always to be smiling, is the Palestinians' political spokesman recognized by 115 UN member nations. But for America, he remains an Invisible Man. He was until early 1980 the one representative whom no one in our government could officially see and with whom no one in our government could officially or even casually talk. This taboo on Palestinians dates from a secret promise that former Secretary of State Henry Kissinger made to the Israeli government. He said the United States would never recognize nor hold talks with anyone in the PLO without Israeli consent.

Andrew Young, while ambassador to the United Nations, talked to the UN's Terzi. On learning this, the Israelis complained to Washington, and President Carter accepted Young's resignation.

Young never alluded to this secret concession to the Israelis. He did say, however, that the "reason for our not having relations with the PLO is probably because of Israel."

While my thoughts wander to Young and the PLO's Terzi, the Jerusalem merchant and Mouhib, I note, are looking at a window display and laughing. It is a warm mid-December day. Terzi has placed a mock Christmas tree, about four feet tall, in his front window. He has decorated it with scraps of paper on which he has incribed in Arabic the various "gifts" he as a Palestinian businessman received from the Israeli occupation.

"You have a saying in your country, nothing is more certain than taxes and death, and we experience both under Israeli occupation," Terzi says. Then he proceeds to read in English the "gifts"from the occupation: several heavy municipal taxes, high income tax, value added tax, security tax, defense tax, successive devaluation of Israeli currency, continual inflation, confiscation of goods, and slow death.

We leave Terzi, retracing our steps along Saladin Street. His thoughts still on the firing of Andrew Young because he talked to a PLO observer, Mouhib recalls the incident of the United States ambassador in Damascus, Talcott Seeley, who "by the sheerest of accidents encountered PLO official Abu Mazin at a reception in the Syrian capital. The United States State Department gave all kinds of apologies and explanations for a purely haphazard, chance meeting. Americans, it seems, can talk to everybody except a Palestinian.

"The United States says it wants peace," Mouhib continues. "There are two parties at war. The United States talks to only one party, the Israelis. You refuse to talk to the Palestinians. I doubt if the president of the United States has ever seen a real, live Palestinian, much less talked to one.

"Americans are broad-minded on almost every issue, it seems, except on the issue of the Palestinians. And there you try to make us an invisible people. You refuse to see that we were always here in Palestine, and that we are still here in Palestine. We have not disappeared, although some Jews say we do not exist."

As Mouhib talks about our penchant for making people invisible, I recall that for several decades we made the people of China invisible, and also for three centuries we made the blacks in the United States an invisible people.

Mouhib, who apparently knows all the Arab businessmen along

Nablus Road, stops to chat with a Palestinian in his mid-forties who stands outside a small office equipped with a chair, table, and telephone. Mouhib introduces me to Anwar, who, on learning I live in Washington, D.C., volunteers that he has two brothers living there.

"Anwar has a reliable taxi service," Mouhib tells me, suggesting I might want to call him sometime.

Maybe, I say, the next time I go to Tel Aviv Airport, I will give him a call. What will he charge? He quotes a price, and it is almost twice what I paid on previous trips when I shared an Israeli taxi with six other passengers. Anwar explains that his price is higher because of a handicap placed on Palestinian taxis. The Israelis stipulate that all incoming passengers ride only in Israeli taxis.

"I can take you out to the airport, but I am not permitted to return with any passengers. Since only Israeli taxis may take passengers going and returning, this eliminates almost all airport business for Palestinians taxis," Anwar explains.

As Mouhib and I leave Anwar and continue our walk back to the American Consulate, Mouhib points out that tourism, which is big business in any large city of the world today, is crucial in Jerusalem because it is a city with very little industrial base. "We have no port, no river, no natural resources, no energy source except the sun. We live in a museum city. About a million tourists come here every year. The majority are Christian pilgrims. But their money goes for the most part to Jewish hotels, Jewish restaurants, Jewish guides, and Jewish cabs.

"It is a cruel pretense for Israelis to claim they have 'united' the city," Mouhib continues. "The Jews cannot 'unite' with us because they built a Jewish state. Since it is a Jewish state, they want only Jews. They once were branded as inferior, and now that they are in charge they single us out as second-class citizens. They brand us in many ways.

"Anwar is one small example. They do not share the business. And also, they tell Anwar he must paint his taxi in a certain way. The Jews can immediately distinguish an Arab taxi. Why must Anwar paint his taxi differently?

"Every Arab car owner is also branded in a certain way—the first three digits of an Arab license plate are different. Israeli police can immediately spot an Arab driver.

"Every Arab telephone owner is branded. Every Arab phone number must have an initial digit eight. We all feel we are monitored.

"They take money in taxes but do not provide equality in services. They issue public telephone directories in Hebrew but not in Arabic.

"They brand us in more important ways. We are not permitted to have any political parties.

"I cannot travel within the country or outside the country without special passes," Mouhib continues. "I can be exiled from my home without recourse to the courts.

"The Jews have made Israel exclusive. If I, for example, should attempt to buy or to rent a flat within Israel, this would be openly opposed by the ministry of housing, the municipality, and by other agencies.

"Most of their land belongs to, or is administered by, the Jewish National Fund. They forbid me as an Arab to dwell in that land— my father's land—or even to open a business on it. I as an indigenous Palestinian am unclean. They are proud to create towns that are 'clean of Arabs.' They like to pretend that there are no Palestinians. To carry out this cruel pretense, they will not call a Palestinian a Palestinian. In all official documents I am not listed as a Palestinian or an Arab but as a 'non-Jew.' I am discriminated against for one reason: because I am not a Jew.

"I do not know of a single kibbutz that accepts an Arab as a member. They allow Arabs only to work." Mouhib relates that he once worked on a kibbutz, and he was one of countless Palestinians who told me this. While he was there, "a Jewish girl fell in love with an Arab worker, and she asked the members to let him join. They fired the Arab and expelled the woman. They say only Jews can live on the kibbutz."

I suggest to Mouhib that since he works for the United States Consulate, he surely must have some special considerations. "No Palestinian does," he replies. "Mayors and laborers, we are all the same. The Israeli military government assumes from the start that every Arab is a security risk, and they monitor and control every aspect of one's personal life and business activities. We constantly are humiliated.

"Once, I hurriedly changed a suit and forgot my identification card. I was stopped at a roadblock, and not having the I.D., I was taken to jail and held as a common criminal. I told them I worked at the American Consulate, and they said they didn't care where I worked. I was not permitted to call my lawyer. Or anyone. Luckily, I was released after three days."

I examine Mouhib's identification card. It carries this notation: "This identification does not represent verification with relation to the law of entry into Israel."

"That means that if I leave Jerusalem or the West Bank I have no assurance that I will be permitted to return," Mouhib explains. "This is true with any Palestinian Arab. The Israelis can by whim refuse reentry to anyone who has gone out. For a thousand reasons, we live constantly in fear."

Once Mouhib and I, with five other passengers, are in an Arab taxi that is stopped at a roadblock. An Israeli soldier comes to the taxi. I watch Mouhib automatically remove his identification card, worn to fragments, and hand it to the soldier, who is heavily armed. He examines the tattered card. Mouhib, no doubt remembering his days in jail, seems to shrink several inches. Will the soldier tell him the card is worthless? Outdated? We wait. The soldier takes a cigarette from his mouth and extinguishes it under his boot. In these moments Mouhib sees himself and also knows that I see him as weak and vulnerable. The soldier bends over and returns the card.

The taxi continues. "We never know," Mouhib comments. No matter who we are, what name we have, what job we hold. We never know."

Leaving Mouhib in East Jerusalem, I hurry to have tea in West Jerusalem with an Israeli, Meron Benvinisti, who had served under Mayor Teddy Kollek as an assistant for Arab affairs and had written a book in which he urged the Jews to be fair with Arabs in occupied East Jerusalem. Over tea, we both agree it is difficult to meet anyone in Jerusalem, Arab or Jew, who tries to be fair, who tries to be dispassionate and is willing to take off blinders and see beyond his or her own myopic view, realizing all the world needs peace between Arabs and Jews. I admire Benvinisti for seeing the big picture and seeing it all so objectively.

After we chat for perhaps forty-five minutes, we both stand to go, and the personable Israeli suggests that since he has his car he can drop me where I'm going. I say fine, he can drop me at the Damascus Gate. We get into his car, and he speeds around the back side of the Old Walled City. We are now inside Arab Jerusalem, and twilight turns to darkness. As we are circling the wall, an Arab traffic policeman whistles Benvinisti to the roadside and says his car lights are defective. Benvinisti reacts as though the honor of his mother is at stake.

"My lights are not defective!" Benvinisti replies, shaking a fist so vigorously that the car rocks beneath us. This is not a question of headlights, but of an Arab questioning a member of a ruling race.

"Get in this car!" Benvinisti orders, and the Arab policeman, frightened and uncertain, crawls like a cowed dog into the backseat. "I'm taking you to the police." Benvinisti announces. We speed off. No one speaks. Benvinisti drops me near the Old City, then races away to the Israeli police headquarters, where the matter of the car lights will be decided on the highest level.

The next morning I relate the incident to an American friend, newly arrived in Jerusalem, who said, "I think it is only natural to be angry, to talk back to a cop." And I agree with that. Yet, I could not help comparing the two incidents I had witnessed the same day—Mouhib, an Arab, stopped by Israeli police, and Benvinisti, an Israeli, stopped by Arab police.

Mouhib, the Arab, was docile and beaten down, and he obediently, wordlessly produced his tattered identification card. He could not argue; he could not say a word. He was surrounded by armed men. One word—and jail. But the Jew could and did talk back to the Arab.

Several Arab policemen in East Jerusalem told me they were only puppets. Mousa, the Arab policeman who on our first encounter had told me he and Jewish police cooperated splendidly, later amended that statement and said with bitterness, "President Carter came to Jerusalem, and the Israeli police chief took away my gun and the guns of all East Jerusalem policemen. They do not trust us."

This is not the first time I have seen puppet policemen. I was in Germany and Japan after their defeats. The Germans and Japanese had police, but the victorious forces were in charge. And I saw arrogant American soldiers, acting as if they were vastly superior to the people whose land they occupied. So one may say that one military occupation is no different from another. But the Israeli occupation is different in that it is the longest military occupation in modern history. And as old al-Hammuri had said, "They don't want to leave. They want to annex the rest of Palestine."

Mouhib has cousins who live in a section of Arab East Jerusalem called French Hill, and one day he and I drive there and I meet Fawzieh Abu-leil, a large woman of about forty wearing a long black Palestinian dress. Fawzieh serves coffee. A sister named Safieh and a half dozen other relatives, with surnames of Obeideh and Odeh, join us.

"We owned a large part of French Hill. And one day bulldozers came and the Jews took our land. Every Palestinian is now afraid to look out his window. We fear we will see bulldozers," Fawzieh Abu-leil begins. Then her sister Safieh speaks:

"We had half an acre and it was fenced, and we had almond trees and some vegetables. The Jews asked for our documents of ownership, which we produced. Then early one morning we saw bulldozers on our land. Our entire family rushed to prevent the bulldozers from plowing under our trees. I threw stones at the bulldozer, and one soldier grabbed me and another hurled me to the ground. By force they evicted us from our land. They are cutting down our trees and taking our land to make a parking lot."

The cousins take us to meet neighbors, an eighty-year-old man named Khalaf and his wife. "The Israelis took hundreds of acres from us in 1948. We owned the land on which the Jews built their Knesset [parliament]. We were forced from West Jerusalem to East Jerusalem and now this home has been condemned," Khalaf, who seems a broken man, relates.

"Here is a petition," says his wife, producing well-worn pages in English. "We and other Arab land owners sent it to the Israeli government." I read a portion: "We are the owners of the land. You have forced us into humility. We are appealing to your heart. We are hundreds of people living in tragedy. We are living on our land. We are told that your government will demolish our homes on land which we have inherited for thousands of years . . ."

After leaving the petition with Israeli authorities, Mrs. Khalaf relates, "We got a short reply: 'We will discuss.' Then, 'to discuss' they sent the leader of their police, who told us to get off the land.

"Earlier, two of our sons, both medical doctors, protested to the Israelis about the confiscation of our lands. The Israelis then arrested our sons and put them in jail. They tortured them and expelled them without trial." Her sons are Dr. Ahmad Khalaf, a mental disease specialist, and Dr. Mohamad Khalaf, a general practitioner. Both are living in Amman, Jordan.

Another neighbor, a Palestinian woman about sixty, tells us: "In 1968, the Israelis took our land without compensation to enlarge their Hebrew University. They came at night with bulldozers. They worked day and night to build. Now my family and sixty-two other Palestinian families will be driven from our homes so that the Jews may enlarge their dormitories. The Jews take our land step by step. We are a sausage and they take us slice by slice."

Mouhib and I also visit clusters of high-rise apartments, called Gilo, halfway to Bethlehem. Here we meet a Palestinian widow, Halime Hassan Abdul-Nabi Sharafat, seventy, who lives under the shadow of one of the skyscrapers built for Jewish immigrants. She shows documents she says prove she owns the land where she lives, as well as other land on which the high-rise apartments are built. "I regularly pay municipal taxes on this property," she says.

From her small garden, I watch a blond, blue-eyed, stylishly dressed immigrant descend the back steps of her modern apartment. The old dark-skinned Palestinian Arab in her long, traditional dress notes the Western immigrant and remarks, "The blue eyes have taken my land." Then she recalls in growing bitterness:

"My husband was shot dead by the Israelis in 1948. I am here alone. I have one son living. The blue eyes are permitted to take my land. But my son in Kuwait is not permitted to return home to Palestine. Once, soldiers came and they shouted to me in Hebrew. They took me to prison and kept me three days. They offered me money and asked me to leave my land. And I said, 'If you offer me all the money in Israel, I will not take a penny. I will die before I leave my house.'"

We also meet another Palestinian woman, Aycha Yassin Abu Taa, who lives in Arab East Jerusalem within a stone's throw of where Prime Minister Menachem Begin said he would move his offices to symbolize Israeli sovereignty over the entire city of Jerusalem, including the Arab sector.

The eighty-year-old woman said Israeli officials visited her and offered her money to move from her house and she told them, "You can fill the house with gold but I will not move. I will die in this house." In 1948, she said, she and her husband and their children were driven by Israeli soldiers from their Arab village of Lifta on the outskirts of West Jerusalem. "Our home was destroyed. Then we resettled on property we owned in East Jerusalem. Then one day my husband went outside and saw Israeli bulldozers. He came back inside and said, 'Our land is gone,' and he died of a heart attack."

As we leave the old woman, Mouhib comments, "She wants to die in peace, but that will not be permitted.

"We Palestinians were not alone in saying the Israelis could not annex Arab Jerusalem. Beginning in 1968, the United States officially stated that the part of Jerusalem that came under Israeli military control was, like other areas occupied by Israel, subject to the provisions of international law.

"When the Israeli government said the annexation of East Jerusalem was a matter of basic Israeli law, Egypt's Anwar Sadat suspended peace talks, because even the most moderate Arab leader cannot go against the beliefs of eight hundred million Muslims who regard Jerusalem as sacred.

"The overwhelming majority of the countries of the world, as well as the Vatican in Rome, have never recognized Jerusalem as the capital of Israel," Mouhib continues. "Almost all foreign embassies, including that of the United States, are located in Tel Aviv. Only three or four small South American countries keep embassies in West Jerusalem, and they probably will move to Tel Aviv. The United States Ambassador in Tel Aviv will not go to Arab East Jerusalem to see a Jewish prime minister there.

"Hundreds of millions of people want Jerusalem to be a sacred city—not a political pawn. Under the 1947 United Nations partition plan, the Holy City was supposed to have been placed under international supervision. It was not to belong to one people, but to all people of the three faiths. Israel's announcement regarding its right to Arab Jerusalem not only embittered Palestinians but Arabs throughout the world, as well as world leaders who recognize that Jerusalem is a key to peace. The Israeli announcement polarized international opinion on the city's status.

"Because Arabs have lived in Jerusalem for millennia and Jews have returned here, and both feel passionately that Jerusalem is their Jerusalem, Arabs and Jews will find reaching a solution on Jerusalem the toughest part of any peace agreement," Mouhib says. "Most moderates in all three faiths agree that the question of Jerusalem is for the end of the peace process, when passions have been cooled by the vision of a new future."

Meanwhile, no one is more passionately fanatical than the Israeli Geula Cohen, the sponsor of Israel's provocative law affirming Jerusalem as the capital, who has said if she cannot live within a Greater Israel that would include Arab East Jerusalem, "I don't want peace." Cohen, who opposed peace with Egypt, added, "The Jews did not come back to Israel to be safe."

The vast majority of Jews undoubtedly disagree. An Israeli chief rabbi, asked if Jewish religious law would require keeping old Jerusalem at all cost, replied: "It's an absurdity! The supreme law of Judaism is to respect one's own life except in two cases: if you are forced to deny God, or if you are compelled to kill another man, in which case better you should die. But otherwise the priority is staying alive. To sacrifice the life of a single soldier for the sake of conquest of Jerusalem is against Jewish law."

Mouhib points out that when the Israelis came "it was the first time a people established a capital in a land that already had a capital—Jerusalem always has been the capital of Palestine. We are striving for peace. We do not ask the Israelis to give up Tel Aviv, nor even West Jerusalem. But we are Palestinians living in East Jerusalem. There are virtually no Jews in East Jerusalem except those like the ones we met—who take Arab land and build modern high-rise buildings. They are enclaves in our Arab community.

"East Jerusalem was the Arab administrative center for the West Bank. It was and is still our Arab cultural center. To the Arabs who have always seen East Jerusalem as our capital, it is inconceivable that the Jews, who have taken West Jerusalem, would now want East

Jerusalem as well. The city may remain open physically, as far as I'm concerned, but we will administer our separate municipality. We will reinstate our Supreme Court, which the Israelis closed in 1967, as well as our government offices. Jerusalem is our largest Arab city on the West Bank and it will serve once more as our educational, commercial, and political headquarters."

With Palestinians in the West Bank

Should you as a visitor suddenly find yourself either in the Gaza Strip or the West Bank, the native people who are Palestinian Arabs would probably ask something like, When did you come to Palestine? The two areas comprise about a quarter of the historical territory of Palestine and are inhabited by about 1.2 million Palestinian Arabs. More than 400,000 live in the Gaza Strip and 800,000 in the West Bank, including 105,000 residents of Arab East Jerusalem. These Palestinians form a third of the Palestinian people. Another half million Palestinians live inside Israel, and more than 1.5 million live in exile in Jordan, Lebanon, and Syria, as well as the United States and other countries.

I traveled throughout the West Bank by Arab bus, almost always alone. In many instances, I felt the eyes of the occupying Israeli soldiers focused on me, their guns at the ready. More than once I was stopped and interrogated. I was more frightened than when I was in actual battle zones during the Korean and the Vietnam wars. There is nothing clean about any war, but neither is there anything clean, peaceful, or relaxed about existing in a land where Israeli soldiers have their guns over a people who are determined to be free of the tyranny of a seemingly endless military occupation.

I went to Nablus, the largest of the West Bank cities, after East Jerusalem, to discuss the future of the Palestinians with the city's Palestinian mayor, Bassam Shaka. This visit was prior to his loss of both legs in a car bomb explosion attributed to Jewish terrorists.

I show up at his offices without an appointment, but after having sat outside for five or ten minutes, I am called in to see him. He rises from his desk and offers me a wooden straightback chair that stands against a wall, and he sits beside me on another straight wooden

chair. His office, I note, is somewhat small, and by Western standards, stark, without carpeting or wall decorations.

Shaka, elected to office in 1976, is about fifty, of medium build,
with light-colored skin, a receding hairline, and a moustache. He
looks overworked, tired, and harassed.

"I expect to enjoy a few days away from my desk. I have been
invited to speak at a Detroit university. I look forward to this trip,"
he says, and for a fleeting moment he seems young again. Then he
adds, "I am waiting for permission to go."

The telephone rings. The mayor's petite secretary, Susan
Rasekh, who sits in the room with us, answers. The mayor rises and
walks to his desk and speaks a few words into the phone. I see the
lines in his face droop, forming an expression I recognize as disap-
pointment. He hands the phone back to his secretary, returns to the
wooden chair beside me, and tells me quite simply that "They"—
meaning the Israeli military authorities—"will not allow me to travel
to America.

"I cannot run my own life or run Nablus as I like. The occupation
forces make little boys out of men. We have to ask permission, to
beg, to plead. We must ask permission for our every move and we
are given permission or refused permission on the basis of our obedience to the authorities and the extent to which we have criticized
the Israeli occupation. I and other West Bank mayors are punished
for speaking against the Israeli military occupation of our land. Yet
we all criticize it. We Palestinians have twenty-five municipal governments in the West Bank and one in Gaza, and without exception,
all are opposed to Israel's continued occupation of our land."

Referring to his telephone call, Mayor Shaka remarks, "I get my
orders like that, in the form of a phone call. Often I do not know the
name of the person. The voice speaks for the military governor. The
voice gives me an order. And I do not get a letter or anything in
writing confirming the order. And when an order does come in writing it is rarely signed by an individual but bears the name, 'The Military Rule.' This makes it difficult for me to know with whom to deal
in their military hierarchy.

"Also, restrictive rules and regulations make fiscal planning and
budgeting especially difficult. We cannot levy any taxes without
prior approval by the Israeli occupation authorities. We continue to

get loans from the Jordanian government, but the Israelis restrict us in collecting the loans. And even when aid money has been deposited in a Nablus municipal account, we cannot spend it as we would like. We must submit a plan, and the Israeli military government must approve this plan. So there are endless frustrations and delays."

The West Bank and Gaza traditionally have been farmlands, but the growth of cities such as Nablus, which now has a population of close to 100,000, means that there are more urban people who need more services, and "the list of all that we need is almost endless. We have no resources such as coal or oil and almost no industry of any kind. Rather than help us, the military forces tie our hands.

"They do not permit us even to prepare our youth," Mayor Shaka continues. "The Palestinian young people have very limited educational and vocational training opportunities. For instance, in all the West Bank, we have only three vocational-technical and teacher-training schools. They provide training for about thirteen hundred students. Thousands more want this training. But our efforts to open more such training schools are blocked. As an example, the city of Hebron asked permission to establish a polytechnic institute. The Israelis kept the application pending for years and then phoned and said, 'No, you can't have a training institute,' and gave no reasons.

"They not only forbid our building new training schools, but also arbitrarily close the few training schools we have. For instance, they closed Ramallah Boys' Secondary School, with five hundred pupils; the women's vocational teacher-training center at Tireh, near Ramallah, with six hundred fifty students; and the Ramallah Women's Teacher-Training Institute, with two hundred sixteen students. They kept these schools closed for most of 1979. The Israeli authorities also shut, for shorter periods, the Hisham Bin-Abdel-Malik Boys' Secondary School in Jericho, with three hundred twenty-eight pupils; and the boys' secondary school at Halhoul, with six hundred pupils.

"Our young people suffer a terrible kind of harassment. Most everyone who gets an education is then forced to work outside. More than one hundred Palestinian engineers have gone from one small village, Denaba, near here, and are now working in Saudi Arabia, Libya, and other Arab countries. Three-fourths of the Palestinians have been forced to leave our country, to study or to work.

"The Israelis want us all to leave," Shaka believes. "They say, 'You should go to Kuwait or Arabia. They speak your language.' Or, 'Go to Jordan. Go to Libya.' That is like telling an American, 'Get out. Go to Australia. They speak your language.' They forget we are Palestinians and not like the Jewish leaders, immigrants from Europe. We insist, we are none other than Palestinians. We have our own personality. We are not from another land. We have always lived in Palestine.

"Now we are a people expelled from our homeland in 1948, and those not expelled are a people grappling with the terrors of a military occupier bent on subjugating us to the rule of the gun.

"At home and in exile we number 3.4 million. We are one, a cohesive, national group with a common culture, traditions, and aspirations. Geographically and historically we are rooted in the same soil and hold the same goals. We stand fast in our love of Palestine. The essence of a Palestinian is his rejection of the idea of exile."

Nothing, Shaka believes, will be more dangerous to world peace than Israel's continued economic colonization of the area. "Our people have been under a yoke of occupation. Now we need air to breathe and an opportunity to work in peace. Most of all, we need regional cooperation to bring about economic development of the area. To have regional cooperation, the mayors and other leaders of the West Bank must plan together, but we are not allowed to hold such meetings.

"Moreover, the West Bank mayors have not been permitted to get help from the United Nations. The UN tried to help. Its General Assembly gave a mandate to a UN Development Program to visit the West Bank and Gaza and establish concrete projects to improve our economic condition.

"However," Shaka continues, "Israel did not permit the UN Development Program into the West Bank and Gaza. As a result, we are totally lacking in economic and social research and planning. We need study programs in fields that include education, health, agriculture, industry, trade, transport, housing, and social institutions. We have been left orphans of the world too long.

"We Palestinians traditionally have been farmers, a rural people. The European Jews who created Israel came with their Western producer-consumer techniques and with the billions of dollars supplied by the United States. They advanced technologically and soon reached a point where they needed foreign markets for their productions. The Israelis became like the British empire, which sold to the colonies it controlled. The Israelis sell to us, whom they control. We have no freedom, no choices to go elsewhere. We buy ninety percent of our imports from Israel, yet Israel takes only about two percent of its imports from the West Bank and Gaza.

"As the occupying power, they restrict exports to our agricultural products that are not competitive to theirs. They promote certain crops within Israel for the benefit of Israeli exports, and they thereby create production patterns that are not compatible with the long-term interest of West Bank agriculture. Overall, it is a classic pattern of colonial economic dominance and exploitation. From the start of its occupation, Israel has increased tenfold its exports to the Palestinians, until the West Bank and Gaza are second only to the United States as Israel's largest export market.

"In any economic development, electricity and water are all-important. The Israelis term me militant because I resist their efforts to make Nablus dependent on Israeli electricity and water," Shaka says.

"In the case of electricity, the Israelis want me to connect the Nablus area with the national grid in Israel and allow them to annex the area electrically. Instead, I have worked to convince the Israeli authorities I should be allowed to import electrical generators. The Israelis must approve all such orders. We place an order. Someone sits on it. And we wait years to get one generator.

"Water is even more crucial, a commodity that can in truth be defined as more precious than oil. We recognize that a primary reason Israeli authorities want to continue their military control of the West Bank is not because of religious reasons or security but because they have a source of water here in the West Bank.

"The Israelis get most of their water from the Sea of Galilee. They began construction for a water pipeline from the Sea of Galilee south through the Jordan Valley in order to support a major expansion of their illegal settlements there and to consolidate their control over water resources. The Israelis have pumped so much water from the Galilee that it is at lower levels than ever before. The small Jordan River flows into the Dead Sea, now so low that it can be crossed by foot at one place. Increasingly, Israel has looked to the West Bank for its water. In fact, the West Bank has become little more than a reservoir for Israel," Shaka claims.

The reservoir actually is rainwater that falls into underground porous rock and sand called aquifers. Wells can be dug into the aquifers and, according to Shaka, the Israelis siphon off an increasing amount of West Bank underground water.

"The Israelis take eighty percent of our West Bank water supply," Shaka says. "First, they pump about thirty percent of our water into Israel. Then they pump about fifty percent of our water, so desperately needed by our Palestinian farmers, into their illegal Jewish settlements here on the West Bank."

But why, I ask the mayor, do the Palestinians not take the water they need from their own source? By what means are the Israelis taking eighty percent of their water?

"By two means," he answers. "They install meters on Palestinian wells already in use by Palestinians. They monitor our supply, not theirs. Then, they do not permit us to dig new wells. But they permit Israelis to do so. The Israelis have dug twenty-five wells, seventeen in the Jordan Valley, all for illegal Jewish settlements.

"The Israeli government provides highly sophisticated water pumping, transport, and storage systems, all for the exclusive use of the Jews.

"Jewish settlers in the Jordan Valley plan to irrigate thirteen thousand acres of West Bank land, and they will use the limited water resources that otherwise would go to Palestinian farmers. These Palestinian farmers can only stand by and watch the Israelis drilling new wells for their illegal settlements. If Palestinian farmers lose eighty percent of their water, they lose eighty percent of their crops," the mayor contends.

Surely, I suggest, he as the mayor can authorize a new well for his people.

"They do not allow us to drill any well," he repeats. "Farmers in the Arab village of El Auja watched their natural spring turn dry because Israelis tapped water from it. Almost all of El Auja's one hundred acres of citrus groves was lost. Jordan offered aid money to fund a well for this village. But the Israeli military would not give permission for the well. If Palestinians want to drill irrigation wells, we are told no. Since 1967, Israel has turned down all our requests.

"They not only refuse us the right to drill irrigation wells, they do not permit us to drill wells for drinking water. As one example, we asked for a permit to drill a drinking water well to the east of Nablus. This is for families—women, children, old people, sick people. They refused to permit us to drill this water well. This is not a human thing to do, to deprive people of water to drink.

"They take these hard measures to secure a stranglehold over all our water resources," he continues. "The imbalance in water allocation is part of a deliberate strategy to drive us from our land and force us to sell it at reduced prices. But such tactics can lead only to resistance and violence."

The Israeli officials with whom I talked said they were convinced they are capable of keeping the Palestinians under control. They say they need to retain ultimate control of West Bank water because so much of their supply within Israel proper is dependent on that region.

"There's precious little of it," one Israeli official said. "And we must have the final say over how it is used."

In my meeting with Shaka, I quote the Israeli official's statement. Shaka replies, "Israel keeps a vast military force over innocent people who want freedom. The United States helps Israel perpetuate its policy of subjugation. You are giving Israel, with a high standard of living, almost as much military and economic assistance as all the other 99.9 percent of the world's people combined. It hardly makes any sense that the Americans earmark almost half of all United States security assistance for less than one-tenth of one percent of the world's people. In the beginning the Americans wanted to help oppressed peoples fleeing Nazism. Now the situation has changed. Israel uses your dollars to oppress Palestinians. The United States aid money goes to help perpetuate their injustices.

"We Palestinians in the West Bank and Gaza now have a quarter of the original Palestine. In this territory we want to live in peace."

Shaka outlines these steps to peace:

An end to the occupation and Israeli withdrawal from the occupied territories, including Arab East Jerusalem.

Removal of the Israeli settlements that, in violation of international law, have been established on Arab land. If Jews want to settle in the Palestinian state, there will have to be a principle of reciprocity—Palestinians will have to be able to settle on Jewish land.

Shaka, like all other West Bank mayors, favors the establishment of a Palestinian state under leadership of the Palestine Liberation Organization (PLO), "the only legitimate representative of our people. It is said that the Israelis fear the establishment of a tiny Palestinian state. But why are they afraid? A people with so powerful an army! A defense must include a people's faith and desire for peace. We Palestinians truly desire peace. Let us hope that talks will start between Israel and the PLO."

Back in Jerusalem, I discuss this same subject—Israeli fears of a Palestinian state—with friends I had come to know through a mutual acquaintance in New York. The friends, Dr. Ezra Spicehandler, who headed Jerusalem's Hebrew Union College, and his attractive, vivacious wife Shirley and I are seated in the King David Hotel having coffee and cake. We discuss the West Bank. Spicehandler, who speaks in a measured, reasonable tone, says he does not believe in a Palestine for the Palestinians, and he gives reasons why such a small country should not be brought into this world: it would have no factories, no resources, no political base. In short, he views it as a baby that could not take care of itself. His wife interrupts to say: "And a Palestinian state would terrify the Israelis."

She does not explain why it would be so terrifying. But she is right. Jews are terrified of letting Palestinians have what the world already has given the Jews—passports, government, a flag, and a nation.

Shortly after my first visit with Mayor Bassam Shaka in Nablus, the Israeli government moved to deport him. In arresting him, the Israelis said Shaka supported terrorism. The charges were based on a remark he is alleged to have made to the coordinator of operations in the territories, Maj. Gen. Danni Matt.

Jailed, Bassam Shaka began a hunger strike. All the West Bank mayors and council members resigned in protest of his arrest.

"We are all Bassam Shaka," another West Bank mayor said during Shaka's imprisonment.

Outcries of "trumped up charges" were heard around the world.

Under pressure from critics at home and abroad the Israelis, after holding the mayor behind bars for twenty-five days, reversed their decision and released him. He returned to Nablus, and resumed duties as mayor.

"One can't imagine the feeling of being arrested and told that you will be deported from your homeland," Bassam Shaka said later, when we visited again. Nablus was the town where he and his forebears had lived "forever." To be deported would be to die.

The Israelis earlier had deported, without explanation or trial, Abdel-Jawad Saleh, mayor of the West Bank town of El-Bira. In the summer of 1980, the Israelis, again with no explanation and no trial, deported Fahd Kawasma, the mayor of Hebron, and Muhammad Milhelm, the mayor of Halhoul.

"We were handcuffed, blindfolded, and without reason exported from our homeland," they said.

Then came the car bombings. The mayor of El-Bira escaped unharmed. But Mayor Bassam Shaka lost both legs and Mayor Karim Khalaf of Ramallah lost a foot. Jewish vigilantes, claiming credit for the car bombings, said, "Our aim is to expel all Arabs" from the West Bank. The Palestinian mayors said, "The Jewish vigilantes get arms from the Israeli government and they have the backing of the Israeli government."

On my initial visit to Nablus I went to meet a Palestinian named Muhammad, one of twelve children, who had invited me to stay awhile in his village home near Nablus. We had agreed to meet on a specified day at 10:30 A.M. in the central square of Nablus and go to his village.

Traveling from Jerusalem, I arrive at the Nablus central square and see dozens of soldiers, all carrying submachine guns. They are accosting Palestinians, asking for I.D. cards. I am overwhelmed by the sight of so many soldiers among the civilians. I think it will make an interesting photo. As I reach down—my camera bag is on the ground beside my feet—I see from a corner of an eye soldiers on nearby roofs watching me through binoculars. I close the bag and walk a distance to a collective-taxi stand and sit, as though waiting for a taxi. I remember that an American woman, Terre Fleener, was arrested and held in an Israeli jail for almost two years for having taken some photos. While in prison she confessed to taking pictures of Israeli beaches and hotels but maintained all along that she had not taken military photos or any photos of military installations.

I walk across the square, still frightened by the armed soldiers and even more by armed civilians who roam the streets with clubs and German Shepherd dogs. I am frightened because the soldiers and the civilians with submachine guns are *right*. We say in America that they are. If Andrew Young says Palestinians are people, he is *wrong*. Therefore, if the *right* people should arrest me and keep me locked up for two years, no American in his *right* mind will question their justice.

In the West Bank, there are two kinds of people: the occupiers and those who are occupied. And for the stranger coming into Nablus, there is one code: you are with the occupiers or you are against them. With the names and addresses of Arabs and my notes on interviews, I could be jailed now and questioned later—much later.

I enter a pharmacy and make a small purchase. Somewhat bolstered by this commonplace experience, I check the square, but, instead of Muhammad, I see the soldiers milling about like a restless sea. I find a doctor's office and sit among waiting patients. Outside the windows I see armed guards on rooftops surveying the central square.

I go once more to the public square, but there is still no Muhammad. Soldiers approach me, interrogate me, and once I show an American passport, allow me to leave. Wondering if my knees will support me, I hurry back into the doctor's office. The doctor whose clinic I have invaded comes out of his office to receive one of his patients. Seeing me, he asks if I am ill. I explain that the soldiers on all the rooftops and in the street frighten me. "They are part of our lives," he tells me. "They are here everyday." I sit in his office until noon. Later, I walk to the bus station and return to Jerusalem, where I find an acquaintance who knows Muhammad.

"He is in jail. He was arrested," the Palestinian tells me. I ask the charges. "There are no charges," he says. "The occupation never needs charges."

I have written at length about the West Bank, but the Palestinians also consider Gaza as their homeland.

On several occasions I visited Gaza, about an hour's drive from Jerusalem. A native Palestinian there told me, "We in Gaza are one with the Arabs of the West Bank." How, I asked him, did the Palestinians, if they recover a portion of their country called Palestine, plan to unite Gaza and the West Bank, which now are separated geographically by a chunk of Israel?

"We will build a corridor from Gaza to the West Bank," he replied.

On my visits to Gaza I did not call on the mayor, Rashad al Shawa, but by coincidence I met him once in Amman, Jordan, where he was attempting to raise funds for a number of development projects in the Gaza Strip and Gaza municipality. "I tried to travel to the West Bank to meet with the mayors of other towns under occupation," he related. "The Israelis, however, did not allow me to visit Arab towns in the West Bank. They permitted me to travel to Jordan, but not to stop in Jerusalem, Hebron, or Nablus. Clearly the Israeli government insists on separating Gaza from the West Bank, but we in the Gaza Strip and the West Bank are but parts of one people with one destiny."

Kareemi,
a Palestinian

Kareemi has none of the sophistication one might expect in the United States from so attractive a young woman. She has dark, shoulder-length hair, a ready smile that moves into dimples, and long, slender legs that fit her jeans the way most women wish theirs would. Kareemi is nineteen, and coming to know her I see her personality constantly change from guileless and shy to confident and assured. This changing of roles gives her a vulnerability, an ambivalence that in the days before women's liberation we called charm and femininity.

I know her in two worlds: in her West Bank home, where her Arab roots go tenfold deeper than my Western-world roots, and where she moves barefoot like her mother in a traditional family lifestyle; and I know her in her university surroundings. She will choose between the restrictiveness imposed by her Islamic world and the freedoms represented by the West and, in particular, the United States. Or perhaps, if she is among the lucky few, she may somehow be able to meld features of her two worlds—the Orient in which she and her forebears have always lived, and the Occident that thrusts itself upon her culture.

Once, to visit her small village of Deir Debwan, I accompany Kareemi on an Arab bus out of Ramallah. We travel for about twenty-five minutes through dry, rocky farmlands with olive groves. The bus stops in the small central square of Kareemi's village. As we get off, Arab youth, among them Kareemi's sister Nidal, fifteen, and a brother, Naser, eleven, greet us.

We walk a short distance up a hill to a hand-chipped, white stone home built by her father, who is one of sixteen hundred Palestinians deported from his homeland by the Israeli occupying forces. I see

148

three women in long, traditional Palestinian dresses sitting cross-legged on a concrete porch in the sun, chatting and sewing. One of them, Kareemi's mother, rises, and, standing tall and wide of girth, warmly embraces Kareemi and me. Going into the rural communities of the West Bank, one meets recent descendants of Bedouins, and they have a common trait: they treat the stranger as royalty. They give the stranger their best. The visitor must feel as comfortable as, or even more comfortable than, in his or her own home.

Kareemi's mother moves automatically into her kitchen to prepare food and drink. She stands at a small stove that operates on bottled gas. The great majority of Palestinians have never known the luxuries of the modern Western world, private cars, electricity, central heating, air conditioning and television. Kareemi and her family, like sixty-five percent of the West Bank Palestinians, are without running water in their homes, and she and her family, like eighty-four percent of the West Bank Palestinians, are without bathrooms in their homes.

As her mother works, Kareemi places a slender arm around her mother's ample waist. I note the contrast between the two women: one young, outwardly modern, who goes to college and speaks four languages, and the other with only three years of formal education, who looks old because she dresses in what we in the West have come to call the old style. She does not rouge her lips or cheeks, she ties her long hair in a bun, and even on a warm day she is outfitted in layers of heavy fabric that cover all but her face, hands, and feet. The two women express a natural, spontaneous warmth for each other. "She is not only my mother," Kareemi says, "she is my best friend. Her name in Arabic is Bahida. This means wonderful and very beautiful. My mother's father was called Ibrahim and was born in this village of Deir Debwan. He was a sheik, a religious man, a counselor, what today we would call a psychologist. His father was named Muhammad and he also was born in this same village.

"My father is named Shihada, and his father was named Amin," Kareemi goes on. "Amin, my grandfather, was lord mayor of this village. He lived under its occupation by the Turks, the British, the Jordanians, and finally the Israelis. So he had long experience with occupying governments. When Arabs in the village had problems, they came to him and he helped them.

"I recall—and this is very much in the Arab tradition—that he had a fabulous memory. He could recite poetry and history and literature he had learned from his father and grandfather. He was very polite and polished in manners. He was considered a learned man. Yet he did not know how to read or write.

"Once, for a period of time, my grandfather Amin moved to Jericho, and a brother and I went to live with him, to go to a good school in Jericho. At that time I considered my father progressive and my grandfather more old-fashioned. And I used to quarrel with my grandfather. He would then tell my father. 'You are spoiling your children,' but my father reminded him, 'But, father, you spoiled us.'

"Amin, in addition to my father, had two sons and one daughter. My aunt told me that Amin always told her she was as smart as the boys, and he sent her, as well as his sons, to the best school in Jericho. It made a big impression on everyone in Jericho that Amin sent his daughter as well as his sons to the best school."

Certainly his view of women as equal to men affected Kareemi's father, as well, of course, as Kareemi.

"Amin lived to be ninety-five. He had a bright, alert mind and was strong to the last minute of his life," Kareemi says, adding that she believes the expulsion of her father, Shihada, killed her grandfather. "He was brokenhearted. He died three days after my father was deported."

Reflecting on her grandfather's view of women as equal to men, Kareemi says she knows that Westerners often say, "Arab men subjugate Arab women," but she adds that it is always a matter of individual men in individual cases, and that in her experience, "Couples who love each other work out what is best for their families." She believes women today "must be smart enough to earn a living. And my grandfather and my father saw the Palestinians had only one alternative: everyone had to get educated. And so that is why my father began urging me and my sisters as well as our brothers to get an education.

"My father always told me that I was as intelligent as my brothers. This might not sound like much to you, coming from America, but here in our country it was different. Women traditionally are taught to stay quiet and get married."

I look around the sparsely furnished stone house that Kareemi's father had built. The walls are bare except for the framed honors given Kareemi in her schoolwork, one stating she earned the highest marks in her class. Her sister, Nidal, and her brother, Naser, both have their heads buried in books.

The father must think often of such a scene. In between visits to their home, I returned to Washington, D.C., and telephoned the father in California, saying I knew his family. "And Kareemi?" He asks first of her. Again I return to Deir Debwan village, and I tell Kareemi of her father's asking first about her, and she looks sad, reminding me he has been gone seven years. "And he hardly knows Nidal or Naser."

After his deportation without trial, Kareemi's father had gone to California and become an overseer for a large Southern California farm and vineyard. As he saved money, he sent first for one, then a second, then a third child. He now has three with him: Muhammad, sixteen, who is in high school; Amin, twenty, who works with his father and attends night school; and Fahima, twenty-four, who majors in both nursing and computer science at Bakersfield University.

Kareemi's mother, in the long absence of her husband and three of their children, uses her faith to sustain her. As we sit in the village home, Bahida at regular intervals disappears from our circle to say her prayers. She remains near enough to touch, yet in the accepted code of conduct in a family sharing one room, Bahida mentally marks off her territory, and others do not intrude. It is as if she has curtained herself off or closed a door. She creates her space as on a stage, and with illusion goes into a mosque. She bows, moves her lips, and drops to her knees in the prescribed motions of her devotions.

Meanwhile, as in other scenes on a stage, Nidal and Naser study their lessons, also moving their lips audibly, hearing as well as seeing the words. And Kareemi and I continue to sit on the floor. We entertain ourselves with our talk. And once, without music—the family owns no radio, television, or record player—Naser performs a lively Bedouin folk dance, all of us applauding as for a floor show.

Later, Bahida joins Kareemi and me—the younger children having fallen asleep on the floor—and we talk late into the night about our lives as women, and how we are alike and how we are different. She asks me how it was, coming to a foreign country, knowing no one, and she asks if the hostel where I stay in Jerusalem has a sitting room, such as the room in which we sit. A room where I might meet people and not be alone. The mother says that even with her children around her she experiences a "deep loneliness" for her husband, and she cannot imagine living alone.

We talk on that eternal question that intrigues women of every nationality, color, and creed: the way of a man with a woman, the way of a woman with a man. Who, I ask Bahida, has it harder in this life, the woman or the man?

"The man," Bahida replies. And she again thinks of Shihada, "forced to leave his land, and having no job and going to a new country and knowing that he had responsibility not only for himself but also for a wife and six children.

"We have a strong, good marriage," Bahida continues. "My happiest time was the time we began our married life. And although it was an arranged marriage, I had seen him and liked him and wanted to marry him. For our honeymoon we went to the upstairs room"—a room that now stands empty—"and we stayed in the upstairs room for seventeen days, scarcely going out."

For seven years now she and Shihada have not seen each other, he in his new world, she in their old. As to the future, Kareemi sighs. "We Palestinians do not know our future. We have no freedom.

"My father will soon be an American citizen. He thinks, because the Jews do not arrest American citizens as readily as Palestinians with no passports, that he can return to Palestine. Meanwhile, our family is split in two, three of my brothers and sisters with my father and three of us at home with my mother. My father wants us all together, but I do not know if he can return to live with us or if he will send for us to join him in America. I hope he can come home," Kareemi said, adding she prefers to stay "in my Palestine."

Bir Zeit University

In the West Bank one can leave Jerusalem in a Mercedes taxi and within minutes see farmers tilling their soil by hand plow and traveling by donkey, as in the days of Christ. Bir Zeit University, where I first came to know Kareemi, is in this ancient setting. It is about thirty miles from Jerusalem, and somehow it seems more like three hundred.

To reach Bir Zeit, one travels north from Jerusalem through a kind of moonscape setting of chalk-white rocky hills and vales. Around a bend is a cameo setting, a village nestling atop a hill, surrounded by the greenery of olive groves and fields of wheat. Three edifices rise above the small stone homes of the two thousand Arab Muslim and Arab Christian inhabitants—the minaret of their Muslim mosque, an imposing tower of a new Christian church, and a three-story, white limestone Bir Zeit administration building with a red tile roof.

I first see Bir Zeit from the backseat window of a small, rickety Arab bus, and when I get out at the university, I feel far from home. Here one does not find railway lines or airports, and never mind asking for a Hilton or a Hyatt. A quick glance and one sees that Bir Zeit is not big and bustling like an American university, with a large complex of buildings and parking lots around a football stadium. It is the main university and cultural center for the entire West Bank, but no symphony orchestra, theater, ballet, or opera troupe has made it to Bir Zeit. It consists of a three-story limestone building, a library building with a few classrooms, and a soccer court. And that's it.

I enter an open door of the main limestone building, once a private home, and I am in a small courtyard with tall pine and pepper trees. I take a seat on a bench, under the shade trees, and watch a passing stream of students and teachers. Most teachers dress casually, are in their thirties, like to be called by their first names, and are almost indistinguishable from the students.

I chat with a young French professor, Frederic Farett. "I heard in Paris about the closing of Bir Zeit by Israeli military authorities because of so-called revolutionary teachings, and I even heard this is where the PLO makes its bombs," he says. "But I find none of that. In fact, Bir Zeit seems quieter than many of our French universities."

I also meet Don Maddox and Steve Boswell, instructors of English literature, and we talk about people we know in Texas, where Maddox and I were born, and in Washington, D.C., which is now home for Boswell and me. "I find the students eager to learn," Professor Boswell tells me. "When I give a grade lower than a B, the student comes in to talk to me about it, asking, 'How can I improve?' A grade is a matter of personal pride and prestige. Everyone in the village knows about it.

"The student feels tremendous responsibility to make good," he continues. "Most Bir Zeit students come from poor farm families, and about eighty percent are on scholarship and could not afford the tuition otherwise. If a student has no scholarship, he or she knows that not only his mother and father are sacrificing but that the whole extended family is chipping in—aunts and uncles and cousins are all making a contribution." I remembered that Muhammad, the student for whom I searched in Nablus, had told me that his father, a farmer, spent three-fourths of the family income to pay for his studies at Bir Zeit.

Also I meet Salim Tamari, who earned an M.A. from a Boston university and a doctorate in a Manchester, England, university; and Lisa Tariki, a native of Afghanistan, who studied in Chicago schools and earned her M.A. at Mills College in California. Professor Tariki, who teaches sociology, tells me Bir Zeit graduates have difficulty finding jobs. "Many who major in sociology will be qualified to become teachers, but most West Bank schools do not offer sociology." A large number of students, however, including Kareemi, study sociology. They are limited in what they can study, since Bir Zeit does not have the faculty to teach many subjects, including law and medicine.

"Out of Bir Zeit's total enrollment of thirteen hundred fifty-nine students, forty-five percent are women, which represents a big change in the Islamic world," Professor Tariki says. "The majority of the students are Muslim, although about ten percent are Christian, and the university is open to all."

Since most of the students are from small, rural communities, they come to Bir Zeit believing it is half as large as the universe. The young men are neat, but by American standards somewhat threadbare, and the young women, having been barefoot on the farm, now graduate to high heels and jeans. None of the students I came to know owns an automobile, a motorcycle, or even a bicycle. They walk to and from villages, and others, such as Kareemi, use either collective-taxis or buses.

For several days I live as a member of Kareemi's family, going with her each day to Bir Zeit. I have heard that Israeli military authorities repeatedly have closed Bir Zeit, which has made the small university famous in academic circles around the world, and I am interested in learning why the Israelis think that Bir Zeit is such a threat. "They claim we organize anti-Israel political activities," an American professor tells me, adding with a chuckle, "My gosh, we can't even organize a class schedule."

Kareemi thinks the answer is simple. "We Palestinians have little to call our own in the way of government, industry, or education. Bir Zeit is Palestinian, and the Israeli military forces hate even the name Palestinian, and moreover they do not want us to think for ourselves. They fear an idea may be more powerful than the gun."

Unlike many American youths who have alternative routes to achieving a higher education, a Palestinian student such as Kareemi has little or no choice. "Other than Bir Zeit we have only two West Bank colleges, one in Nablus and another in Bethlehem," she explains. "The Nablus college gets money from Muslims, and Bethlehem University gets its money from Roman Catholics in Rome. Bir Zeit is our own. It is Palestinian. So we feel most at home here."

"Bir Zeit had a simple beginning," Dr. Hugh Harcourt, one of Kareemi's professors, tells me. "A Palestinian family named Nasir in 1924 turned their home into a private grade school. The grade school expanded to become a college and then a university, with one of the Nasir sons, Hanna, as its president."

Dr. Harcourt, tall, slender, scholarly, gray-haired, and deliberate—measuring his words between puffs on his pipe—was born in 1930 in Joliet, Illinois, grew up in Portland, Oregon, and earned graduate degrees in Edinburgh, Scotland, and the University of Copenhagen in Denmark.

Before coming to Bir Zeit, he taught at the American University of Beirut, founded as a Protestant missionary institution and chartered by the New York State Board of Regents. The American University in Beirut is one of the oldest of the Middle East universities, and Bir Zeit is one of the newest.

"Students and faculty here face terrible difficulties," Dr. Harcourt says. "The Israelis have never wanted Palestinians to get educated. Or to have a Palestinian university. They wanted to eliminate Bir Zeit. To do so, they began by striking at its founder and president, Dr. Nasir.

"Israeli soldiers came to his home at midnight. They gave no explanation to him or his family. They handcuffed him and blindfolded him and put him in a truck and drove him to the border and escorted him across. That was it. The Israelis never filed any charges against Dr. Nasir. They treated this American-educated physicist and distinguished intellectual like a criminal. And he has been forced to live outside his homeland ever since, an exile in Jordan.

"Palestinians have little or no academic freedom," Dr. Harcourt continues. "Any kind of organized political activity is completely illegal. Demonstrations are completely illegal. Any kind of assembly of more than five persons is illegal. Any kind of printing, any kind of handbill or poster on any political issue is illegal. If I write an article for publication—and this is true for every teacher, every student—it is censored.

"We are censored on every item of purchase at Bir Zeit. All our books are censored. We select book titles from a Hebrew University catalogue—books, in other words, available to Jewish students, and most of these are denied us. The Israeli censors have declared the more than one thousand Arab publications available in Jerusalem bookstores forbidden to us. Most newspapers printed in East Jerusalem and circulated there are banned here.

"Riad Amin, an Israeli Palestinian, formerly taught here at Bir Zeit. Amin is a Ph.D. candidate at the Hebrew University in Jerusalem, one of about five hundred Palestinian students there. He wrote a book that demonstrated the need for a junior college for the Palestinians in the Galilee area of Israel. The Israelis are opposed to any college for Palestinians. Since Amin wrote that book, the Israeli authorities have denied him permission to continue teaching at Bir Zeit. He cannot even obtain permission to visit the West Bank.

"Even worse," Dr. Harcourt continues, "the Israeli army uses Jewish religious zealots to move in and take repressive measures against the students. It seems they deliberately want a confrontation. I have seen them move onto this campus with their guns and start shooting.

"One such example occurred on May 2, 1979. The fanatics from Newi Tsuf moved onto our campus and deliberately provoked the students.

"One of the settlers, whose name is a matter of court record, shot a twenty-year-old student, Riyad Nakhleh Daoud, in the chest—fortunately not fatally. Students poured from their classrooms. The army moved in, lobbed tear gas, and sealed off the campus. They took one hundred forty students to prison, beat them, and forced them to sign confessions saying they had participated in a demonstration against the Israelis.

"Meanwhile Israeli soldiers searched all buildings and classrooms and found nothing, no weapons, explosives, not even any literature. Nevertheless, the Israelis closed the university.

"They said 'for security reasons.' They can close the West Bank's leading university on 'security' grounds that would not satisfy the ruler of South Africa."

Closed in May 1979, Bir Zeit was not reopened until September of that year. Dr. Harcourt believes "pressure" on the Israeli government from concerned persons around the world forced it to reopen the university. "A call came through to our acting president, Dr. Gabi Baramki, and a voice said it represented the military government, and 'you can reopen,' and that was it. No apology. No explanation for closing, no explanation for reopening."

On another day, a day to which I have alluded in the prologue to this book, I am again on the campus, talking with students who gather between classes in the sunshine on small bleachers at their soccer court. I am in a cluster of a half-dozen women students, and we discuss the difficulties of their participating in the student council activities. We see a student we all know, Ghassan Alkateeb, who is president of the student body, and I ask, When will a woman be president of the student body? A friend, Theresa, explains that "it is difficult because we must allot so much time for study, and then our mothers expect us to help in household duties." Suddenly, I am aware of shouts and screams, and I see Israeli soldiers pouring onto the campus, throwing tear gas and firing shots into the air.

The women students and I jump from the bleachers and frantically run toward the library. I am aware that three soldiers have Ghassan Alkateeb pinned to the ground and they are beating him. And then I am knocked down and a soldier with a rifle—it somehow looks like a bayonet that will pierce my throat—is standing over me and his face and body loom in gigantic proportions, as in some horror movie. I want to speak to him, to say that I am a good person and that he should not kill me, but I also know that Ghassan and others like him might like to say those words and that blood is covering the ground near him—and near me.

And then, as I have related, an Israeli officer, who seems to be in command, runs up and sees the soldiers who are beating Ghassan and says nothing, but then he looks at me and apparently sees that I have light skin and blue eyes and that I do not look Palestinian, and he speaks in Hebrew to the soldier standing over me, words that I take to mean, Be careful, she is a foreigner. At that moment the soldier raises the butt of his rifle. I scramble to my feet, fall, get up again and, following a stream of students, run toward the library. Once inside the door, I run head-on into the librarian who, hearing that Bir Zeit is being "attacked," has the presence of mind to lock the door. I run upstairs to a second-floor window and from this position I see the students fleeing into classrooms to hide. Again I see Ghassan Alkateeb, and he is still pinned to the ground in a stream of blood.

Theresa, tears streaming down her face, grabs me, as for protection, shouting: "There goes Gabi!" We watch the acting president, Dr. Gabi Baramki, walk toward some soldiers, who seem to be officers, holding out his hands, indicating he wants to talk, and I see a soldier slap his face and knock him to the ground.

Suddenly I see the soldiers move toward parked automobiles that are owned by university professors, including Marshall Gunslman, an American professor of education. Using their rifle butts they smash the windows of all the cars. Eventually, the soldiers leave.

Like frightened animals, Theresa and the other students and I come from hiding. Theresa and I are so shaken we can hardly walk.

Two days later, in response to inquiries about the soldiers moving onto the campus, the Israeli military authorities said yes, they sent the soldiers there, and yes, an Israeli soldier had struck the president of the University, Dr. Baramki.

They said, however, they felt no need to hold an inquiry into the behavior of the soldiers. They were acting "according to instructions" and, they added, only "reasonable force" had been used.

Some days later I visit with my Jewish friends, Aviva and Reuven Neuman, and Reuven's son, Simon, by his first marriage, comes unexpectedly for a visit. He is in the Israeli Army. I look up and see not a human being but a uniform, and I automatically stiffen and shrink, and feel like running to hide, as if he were one of the soldiers who had attacked the students and me at Bir Zeit.

Simon goes immediately to shower and reappears in shorts and T-shirt. You look different, I tell him.

"I feel different," he says, smiling.

Somehow, I feel I "love" Simon. Aviva, to whom I feel closer than to Reuven—although I like them both—has a son, Danni, by her first marriage, and she admits she feels closer to Danni than to Simon. She tells me, "Simon and I never hit it off." Simon, however, has a sweet nature. I perhaps love him because I need to love the soldiers who raided Bir Zeit, and Simon is one I can reach—and touch.

A Palestinian Refugee Camp: The West Bank

It is predawn, and Sameetha has overslept. Bashir, her husband, calls her. He speaks in Arabic: "Come on, you've overslept. Get dressed. Make my coffee. I must be off to work."

I do not understand the Arabic words, yet I understand his tone, gestures, and the diurnal pattern: Bashir rises early; Sameetha wants to sleep.

Bashir, forty-eight, thinks his job important. For three decades he has lived in the refugee camp, and he has been out of work as often as not. Now, through a United Nations agency, he has a porter's job. With a protective leather pad on his back, he hoists and carries steamer trunks, huge bags of produce, or pieces of furniture. As a one-man moving van, he earns the equivalent of fifty dollars a month.

Sameetha and Bashir are the parents of five children, the youngest named Nahla. Meeting Nahla, who is sixteen, I at once feel an affinity for her. Like Kareemi, she is tall and slender and has dark hair and dark eyes. Unlike Kareemi, she is painfully shy, turned in on herself, even furtive, like an animal in a cage. About her there seems to be the humility that comes with knowing you are living in a very limited space belonging to others who are more powerful than you.

I come to know Nahla in this way. I am visiting on the Bir Zeit campus and mention to one of Kareemi's professors, Lisa Tariki, that I would like to live awhile in a refugee camp. "No problem," she replies. "We have many students here who live in refugee camps." And she introduces me to Ahmad, twenty, a scholarship student, who is Nahla's brother. It came as a surprise to me that Palestinians from refugee camps were at Bir Zeit. Until then I had somehow imagined all the refugees were removed from the mainstream of life, perhaps like Indians on United States reservations whom we Anglos for so long kept hidden from sight.

I talk with Ahmad, and he agrees at once that I will be welcome in his family's home. About a week later we meet in Ramallah. We walk along streets crowded with Arab Palestinians, looking into shop windows filled with TVs and even commodes, and I realize anew that the world is divided between those who can buy and those who cannot. Then we board an ancient bus and after a fifteen-minute ride get out on the outskirts of town and walk a short distance to the camp.

Entering the refugee camp, I feel I am entering some medieval ghetto. I walk along a narrow alleyway, skirting an open sewage ditch. I pass tens of dozens of one- and two-room houses, each leaning on the other for support. I am in a ghetto without streets, sidewalks, gardens, patios, trees, flowers, plazas, or shops—among an uprooted, stateless, scattered people who, like the Jews before them, are in a tragic diaspora. I pass scores of small children, the third generation of Palestinians born in the ghetto that has almost as long a history as the state of Israel itself. Someone has said that for every Jew who was brought in to create a new state, a Palestinian Arab was uprooted and left homeless.

We enter the door of a dwelling, not distinguishable to my eyes from hundreds of others like it, and I see two women on their hands and knees, both in shirts and pants, scrubbing a concrete floor. They rise, one somewhat laboriously, as she is heavy with child, and the other, the mother of Nahla and Ahmad and other sons, a woman made old before her time by endlessly making do in a makeshift home, a home that is only this room with a concrete floor and blankets stacked against the walls for beds. And, for a toilet, a closeted hole in the floor. Nahla has never known the convenience of a tub or a commode, nor do any members of her family enjoy that greatest of all luxuries, a room or even space into which one can for an hour or a few moments of each day retire, and in solitude meld mind, body, and soul.

The United Nations provides funds to meet basic needs, such as medical clinics and schooling. But no one has extended the kind of help that would allow people like Sameetha and Bashir to somehow help themselves, to somehow propel themselves into a bigger space, a fuller life. Americans, for example, annually give five hundred and twenty-eight dollars per capita to Israelis and three dollars per capita to the Palestinians.

"We are only seven," Nahla comments the first evening, as we sit on the floor. Members of the family—in addition to Nahla, her parents, and her brother Ahmad, include her eldest brother Zayid, twenty-four, a construction worker, and his wife, Rima, nineteen, who is nine months pregnant. Nahla has two other brothers, Abdul and Salah, who are not at home. She does not tell me immediately, but in time Nahla says they are both in Israeli prisons.

Living with Nahla and her family, I am astonished both by their poverty and also by their will to survive under the weight of being a people without a political party, a government, a land, a people without an identity and without a promise for tomorrow. I learn they unite through the shared experience of exile. Once Nahla introduces me to an old man in the alleyway near her home, and she tells me he is the head man of the camp, having once been a village *mukhtar* in the area of Lydda. Her parents and others like them from Lydda wandered from camp to camp until they found this old man, their *mukhtar*, and other friends from home and then they set up the same kind of community, as best they could, that they had known before the 1948 war that disrupted their lives.

I sit beside Nahla listening to her read her English lesson. On all sides I hear a cacophony of radios, loud voices, and wailing babies. Nahla, like every child in this camp, is handicapped in her attempts to study. Moreover, Sameetha constantly asks Nahla's help in household chores. She has no time to think or plan a future outside the camp.

"I feel buried here," Nahla tells me. "I know there is a world out there"—and her eyes seek space beyond the ghetto walls.

Nahla's family does not own a television set, but hundreds of camp refugees do, and Nahla sees, in regularly rerun Hollywood movies, luxurious homes with carpeting and bathrooms and kitchens, and a thousand amenities missing in her life.

For so young a person, she seems uncommonly perceptive about human nature and the unnaturalness of the crowded conditions in which she lives.

"My brothers knew when I began my period. Living so close,

none of us is ignorant about the changes in our bodies, about life," she confides, adding that often she must undress before Ahmad and that he trains his eyes not to see, psychologically, what in truth he sees. "Once, removing my dress I deliberately studied his face. I saw that his features did not change. I knew he was 'not seeing.'" Only in this way, she explains, does each member of the family give the other a sense of space, of living in a room of one's own.

Nahla hopes to go beyond the nightmare of her parents' past. And she has one dream—to continue her education, and then—her eyes widen at the possibility—to leave the camp and get a job. I ask casually, What kind of a job? And then I realize I am thinking of Nahla and her future as if she were living in America, in a land that still provides alternatives. But I am in Nahla's world, where as many as three generations are born in a cramped room, and their only alternatives are to survive or not survive.

Also, I am in a world where women have traditionally never left home, and those who work outside the camp are liberated only to the point of being "free" to labor in Israeli factories and return to what is too often called woman's work.

I watch Sameetha, seated cross-legged on the concrete floor, mixing flour and water, and kneading dough into flat, round, pizza-sized loaves. She has only a hot plate, no oven. She must send the loaves outside her home to be baked.

For meals, we sit on the floor around a low table. We do not use spoons, knives, or forks. At each meal, Sameetha distributes freshly baked bread loaves, the main staple at all meals. I place my loaf on my lap, tear off a chunk and use it to spoon up spicy crushed chickpeas with garlic sauce. I lift small bits of food such as olives, eaten at most meals, with the fingers of my right hand. Sometimes we eat sliced cucumbers seasoned with mint and mixed with thinned yogurt. Most frequently, we dip chunks of bread first into a bowl of olive oil—a big staple in the diet—then into another small bowl of thyme.

Once, we are all sitting on the floor, eating. Sameetha brings a pot of hot tea. As she bends to serve, Bashir inadvertently turns and hits the pot, sending the boiling tea pouring down Sameetha's thighs. She screams, curses, and slaps Bashir, who cowers like a beaten animal.

"Get the paste!" Sameetha shouts to Nahla, who runs to a small cardboard box of possessions and returns not with a medication but with the only salve they have, a tube of Crest toothpaste. Sameetha, still grimacing in pain, lifts her skirt and Nahla applies the paste.

After supper, Sameetha sits on the floor before an old sewing machine with no legs. She motions to a space beside her on the floor, and she shows me how she changes a bobbin, threads the machine, and turns its wheel. She is using these gestures to tell me that the storm—with her angry unleashing of words and her blow at Bashir— is past, and she and her husband will continue to care for the family and continue in the way they know to survive, and that her striking out at Bashir was her desperate attempt to hit not him but the fate that had brought them to this level.

Often Sameetha conveys a hatred for Bashir. Or rather, a hatred for what life has done to him. In more than three decades, Bashir, who looks twenty years older than his age, has never been able to find himself, which is to say he has never been able to find a means to extricate himself and his family from the slough of poverty and despondency in which they seem mired. He comes home from his porter's job looking demeaned, brutalized. He reminds me of a bewildered Navajo Indian I once saw in a crowded city. Separated from his land, the Navajo lost his sense of Indianness, his sense of self. Now Bashir, separated from his "mother earth"—an expression both the Navajos and the Palestinians repeatedly use—feels orphaned, alien, lost.

I meet other men who feel brutalized by living in the camp. They talk of their villages where they "grew up and laughed." Laughter is only a remembered experience. Ibrahim, the baker, is an example.

I accompany Nahla, with a tray of pie-shaped dough, to a small shop where refugees pay a few pennies to get the dough baked. I find myself in a cramped, dark room with a low ceiling. The room is filled with smoke and seems like a dungeon. Ibrahim, a stooped, dark-skinned man of about fifty who seems at the end of his tether, says he starts to work at 5:00 A.M., finishes at 7:00 P.M. and bakes about a thousand loaves a day.

"I am on my feet all day, my legs ache, and my head aches from the smoke, fumes, and heat. I work fourteen hours a day to make enough to feed my family. My health, perhaps also my mind, is breaking from the strain. The camp produces one generation after another of people who are trapped."

Is he training his eldest son, I ask, to take over as baker?

"I am trying to teach him to get out of this camp!" he bellows, as if I have hit his sorest nerve. His eldest son is named Fouzi. He is seventeen and has been invited to Russia to study art.

"Wherever he goes," Ibrahim says, "I am glad to see him escape from the camp."

Walking back to her home, I ask Nahla: Is Ibrahim a Communist?

"I don't know. The Communists reached in to help him," Nahla replies, adding, "Many Israelis claim that if we recover a portion of our Palestine we will create a Communist state. But I do not think so. We are Muslim, and there is a big difference between the beliefs of our religion and Communism."

One morning I walk with Nahla to her school, and she shows me several of her classrooms and takes me to the office of one of the administrators, a Palestinian in his late fifties, who invites me to stay for a coffee. Nahla leaves us, and the administrator begins by telling me he earned degrees in Boston and Chicago universities, and that he was a teacher "in Palestine" before the creation of Israel.

"This is one of ninety-four schools for thirty-five thousand refugee children on the West Bank," he tells me, adding that West Bank and Gaza refugee schools, as well as all Palestinian refugee schools in the Middle East, have for three decades been operated by the UN Relief and Works Administration (UNRWA).

"Overcrowded classrooms are our worst problem. We have not been permitted by Israeli authorities to build new schools since they occupied the area in 1967. Our school population, now more than one thousand in this school, has more than doubled. Consequently, we have to use our schools on double shifts.

"Censorship is another problem," he continues. "We made a list of 117 textbooks we think necessary for the elementary and preparatory cycles. But the Israeli government censored 42 of these. As a result, our students in several courses must rely entirely on classroom lectures.

"About ninety percent of our resources come from voluntary contributions by governments," he continues. "The remaining ten percent is provided by the UN. The Arab countries saved us from bankruptcy in 1979 when Saudi Arabia provided the money we needed at the last minute. But the Arabs believe that the refugee camps were created by the West, and that the Western countries must finance UNRWA."

The administrator pauses to sip his coffee, and I glance around his office, bare save for his desk and three chairs. I see no wall decorations, no photographs, diplomas, or books. What, I ask, does he need most? It is a perfunctory question, and, pencil poised, I await a perfunctory answer, such as, We need more books. But he is done with discussing school needs as such.

"Our freedom! Our freedom!" he replies fervently. "We are a people exiled and held under a yoke of tyranny. We number nearly four million. Three million of us now live in exile—in the West Bank and Gaza, as well as in Jordan, Lebanon, Syria, the Persian Gulf countries, and in scattered groups throughout the world. Only six hundred thousand of us remain in that part of Palestine that became Israel.

"About half of the Palestinian people living outside Israel are still considered refugees, and about twenty percent continue to live in refugee camps. In our refugee school, I see the psychological effect of the prolonged stays in camps: an atrophy of initiative, an increased tendency toward passivity and fatalistic attitudes. It seems contradictory to say our young students are passive, with loss of self-confidence and increased dependence, and at the same time to say that they have mounting drives of vengence. But their hatred builds on their lack of freedom. Israel forcibly produces a generation of tongueless people, and we will, in the end, speak with fire.

"For thirteen years, the Israelis have chosen not to hear us and not to see us. An Israeli premier, Golda Meir, said 'There are no Palestinian people.' But ignoring us does not make us go away. Nor will the Israelis prevent our attaining national independence. Since Israel became a state scores of nations have won national independence, including some that number no more than a few hundreds of thousands. No power on earth can stop a people from throwing off foreign rule, once they have made up their mind to do so. Israel with all its guns and power will not stop us.

"The Israelis give two reasons for not allowing refugees to return to their homeland," the administrator continues. "First, the Israelis say the Palestinians who returned home would create a problem of security in case of war with the Arab states. But Palestinians within Israel are peaceful and quiet compared with Nahla and the thousands like her trapped in refugee camps. The Palestinians within Israel do not wish to be punished or expelled. The refugees such as Nahla, however, have nothing to lose. She will risk life itself to escape.

"The Israelis say, as the second reason why they will not permit Palestinians to return to their homeland, that to do so would make Israel bi-national and they don't want that. They want the state to remain a Jewish state. This I believe is the real reason why the Palestinians expelled from their homeland have never been permitted to return. And it is a valid one if the state must remain Jewish. The Zionists from the beginning, although they themselves were secular, wanted a totally Jewish state. This is why they felt forced to drive out the Palestinian Arabs in 1948. And that is why they rejected the Palestine Liberation Organization's solution of a democratic state in which Jews, Christians, and Muslims would have equal rights.

"High school students are among the most politically active in the West Bank," the administrator says. "In America, high school students, even college students, are not politically aware, especially nowadays. Here, on the contrary, students are the most vocal group. The high school students are much more numerous and more visible. Teenagers originate almost all the demonstrations and protests. They are very politically aware, and the teenage girls, particularly, are always out demonstrating."

Nahla, he continues, helped stage a demonstration on the school grounds. "It was at the time of the arrest by the Israelis of the mayor of Nablus, Bassam Shaka. She and other teenagers marched near the school one day carrying a placard stating, 'We are Palestinians. We must be free.'

"Six armed men who spoke Hebrew—later identified as religious zealots from a new nearby Jewish settlement—jumped from a car and chased them onto the school grounds. They fired their pistols and rifles around the students who were in class.

"The assailants chased Nahla and the other girls from the school into the refugee camp and began throwing stones at women and children who were outside their homes. They even threw stones at one woman who was holding her six-month-old infant in her arms. She ran into her house, but the attackers threw stones through her windows and fired shots into a water tank on the roof.

"The civilian religious zealots left. Then Israeli soldiers carrying guns rushed onto our school grounds and arrested Nahla and other teenagers and kept them in jail for two days."

Later, when I ask Nahla about the arrest, and whether she and her family have felt humiliated about her having been in jail, she replies, "No. Nowadays it is kind of a badge of honor."

That evening, Nahla and I walk with Rima—her face chalk white—to a nearby clinic, where Rima gives birth to a boy, whom she names for her husband, Zayid. Rima returns home the next day. There are only 293 hospital beds available for all the refugees in all the West Bank camps—one for every thousand. And there is only one doctor for every ten thousand refugees.

Zayid looks like all newborn babies, amazingly small and fragile. Yet Rima and the other members of the family insist I hold him and join them in their celebration. They all accept another mouth to feed as a marvelous gift of God. And where will his life end?

Bashir and Sameetha had come to the camp as teenagers, had married, had five children, and had now become the grandparents of a child born in the camp. And would the child in two decades foster more children in this same camp?

We in the West are easily critical of those in refugee camps who have many children. Such families have few amenities and forms of recreation save perhaps, the finest of all—building a family and surviving through the strength of that family. The diaspora of the Jews and their suffering in ghettos did not destroy their families. Neither has the diaspora of the Palestinians and their suffering in refugee camps destroyed the strength and unity of their families.

Nahla learns poetry by heart, and one evening she quotes a poem by a Palestinian, Tawfiq Zayad, as expressing her determination to live, free of occupational forces.

> As if we were a thousand prodigies
> Spreading everywhere
> In Lydda, in Ramallah,
>   in the Galilee . . .
> Here we shall stay,
> A wall upon your breast,

> And in your throat we shall stay,
> A piece of glass, a cactus thorn,
> And in your eyes,
> A blazing fire.

The walls of the room have one decoration, a calendar with a drawing of olive trees. Nahla takes the calendar from the wall and translates its Arabic inscription:

> I believe in a tomorrow.
> And in the struggle;
> I have faith in olive trees.

She explains the olive tree represents the future and the past of the Palestinians. "The olive tree has strength because of its long, tough roots. Our Arabic literature mentions the olive tree as the cure of all diseases, and in the holy Koran, the Prophet Muhammad says, 'Take care of the holy olive tree; from it you will gain your benediction.' The color green and the olive trees represent our future. We have roots here. This we know is our homeland."

That evening Bashir tells a story he must have repeated many times. The year is 1948.

"We were about fifty thousand Palestinians living in and near Lydda [near the present Tel Aviv airport].

"The fighting raged around us, and we saw the Israelis advancing. We heard shouts and an Israeli soldier told us they were ordered not to leave any Arab civilians at their rear—to leave no one in or near Lydda. The Israeli soldiers at gun point drove us out." The decision to drive out the Palestinians, he adds, had been taken by David Ben-Gurion, one of Israel's founders and its first prime minister.

"We were all villagers and none of us, none of the people like my mother and father or anyone in my family, had ever owned a gun, nor did I know anyone who was a soldier. We had nothing to do with the war or the struggle of the European Jews to find a homeland. Yet we were being collectively punished.

"I was same age as Nahla—sixteen—and I remember the armed Jewish soldiers encircling our home and firing shots and shouting in Arabic that they would kill us if we did not leave at once. Yet no one obeyed; it was as if we felt ourselves tied to our soil. Soldiers dragged women by their hair, and my father shouted he could not leave his garden, his trees, and a soldier knocked him to the floor. I had a pet lamb, and I ran to hold the lamb. I was not thinking of my mother or father or our home but of that small animal.

"I watched families fleeing as from a fire, and soldiers shot around them and over their heads, driving them like cattle. Soldiers pushed us out of the house with their guns. We soon found ourselves among thousands of women and children. Some old men could barely walk and mothers carried babies in their arms, and led small children. The children were crying and begging for water, all of us fleeing we knew not where. No one was given time to collect even the necessities, no food or provisions. I mindlessly grabbed my baby lamb, and another neighbor boy carried a pigeon. On the first day of the march I lost my little lamb. Others carried a chicken, a blanket, or a sack of flour that represented their entire possessions on this earth. My mother begged to return to her village to recover her small stove, her few heirlooms, but she was forced to keep moving. On the third day I saw my mother fall. I thought she had fainted. I felt her heart and she was dead. Then later, my father died. The other Palestinians dug holes in the ground and buried first my mother and then my father. I saw many old people and children fall and die because of the heat and exhaustion."

He sighs deeply, and goes on, "One day we were Palestinians living in Palestine; the next day we were Palestinians driven from a land called Israel.

"We were tens of thousands kicked out by force, our villages destroyed. Even the Jews admit there is not a single Jewish village in their country that is not built on the site of an Arab village. They built the Jewish village of Nahala on the Arab village of Mahloul, and the Jews built Gifat on the Arab village of Jifta.

"They drove us out, they bulldozed our homes, and they built new villages.

"In 1948 I lived in one of about six hundred Arab villages in the part of Palestine that was taken by Israelis. My village was one of about five hundred bulldozed and destroyed. Now you will not find more than one hundred Arab villages left in the part of Palestine taken by the Zionists. The Israeli leaders admit they did this. They are not ashamed. They do not try to undo what they did to us. They justify their acts and glorify them."

Once again he speaks of his family's farm and admits he was never able to find himself, "living on a slab of concrete. I tried—but I failed. Now my spirit is gone."

He looks to Nahla as he talks, wanting her to understand his burden and hers. Bashir knows he is spent by life, but he says, "Nahla, you, and others like you, will make the struggle."

Zayid, a Palestinian Worker in Israel

Always, traveling in the West Bank, I am in towns and villages that are inhabited exclusively by Arabs, and thus the question comes to mind, Why would the Jews, who have created an all-Jewish state, want to militarily hold the Arab West Bank? Nablus Mayor Bassam Shaka gives one of the reasons: the Israelis take water from the West Bank. And they have grown dependent on that water.

Zayid, Nahla's oldest brother, provides another reason: the Israelis get a cheap and flexible work force—of which Zayid is a part—from the West Bank, as well as from Gaza. And they have grown dependent on that work force.

Zayid, husband of Rima, father of the infant Zayid, and the real breadwinner in Nahla's family, has brown hair, green eyes, and a strength that conveys an image of a Mack truck, heavy, low to the ground, durable. He needs no alarm clock. He rises at 3:30 A.M., dresses silently, moves with animal-like quietness, and is out of the house within minutes. At 3:45 A.M., Zayid boards a truck parked outside the camp. Along with dozens of other workers from the camp and surrounding villages, he stands in the back of the truck for more than an hour as it delivers him and other Arab workers into Israel.

Zayid is typical of the Palestinian work force in Israel on many counts. He is twenty-four, and most of the Palestinian workers in Israel are young, from eighteen to thirty-five. Most, like Zayid, are unskilled or semiskilled. Most, like Zayid, say they go to work for the Jews because they have "no choice."

In the West we are suspect of that phrase "no choice," and we tend to think the person using it is lazy or inept. And we think so because we ourselves have choices. Zayid was not, of course, born in the West, but in a land he calls Palestine, where for thousands of years his forebears were farmers, and today Zayid has "no choice," no chance of being a farmer in Palestine because the land that was his father's is now occupied by Jews. And he has "no choice" about going to work at a West Bank Palestinian factory because the Israelis control the economy and do not give permits to the Palestinians to build factories. "We have a few cottage industries but not a single factory on the West Bank," Zayid says.

Thus, Zayid is one of eighty-five thousand Palestinians who each day cross the line and provide a cheap and flexible work force for Israel. "We take any job they offer," Zayid says, and he runs through a mock conversation of an Arab employee with an Israeli employer: Do I want to scrub pots and pans? Oh, yes! Mow a lawn? Wash your floor? Why, of course! Collect garbage? Clean a dairy barn? When can I start!

"I try anything. I worked as a busboy in a Jewish restaurant, I scrubbed floors in a Jewish hospital, I ran an elevator in a Jewish office building, and I even cleaned a Jewish slaughterhouse. I began working for the Jews when I was fourteen.

"Most Arabs start working for the Jews as I did, on a kibbutz. I was one of about twenty-five Arabs who worked there. We did the planting and harvesting—the bend-and-stoop labor.

"Many Jewish immigrants come to Israel from large European and American cities and they have no tradition or training or affinity for the soil. But I enjoyed the farm work. And this was because as a child I heard my father talk of his farm land and he said the soil was our 'mother earth.' So when I got near the soil, I immediately knew an affinity, a kinship. And whatever tasks I was assigned I felt happy because I was near the plants and sky and earth. I like being out of doors, even in the rain or heat or cold. I enjoyed planting and harvesting, even when I knew that I was doing it for the Jews.

"After the kibbutz, I worked six months in a canning factory, and, for awhile, in the packaging of foods. All my co-workers were like me, transported in from the West Bank. I saw so many Arab workers in the plants, I decided the Israeli food industry must be totally dependent on Arab workers. The food industry has peak and slow periods, and in the slow periods we Arabs are the first to go." Laid off from the canning factory, Zayid found employment in a Tel Aviv mattress factory.

"Tel Aviv is an all-Jewish city, and they have rules about wanting to keep it 'clean of Arabs.' We are permitted to go into Tel Aviv only to work. Entering, we must show our work permit. But the work permit is not good to stay overnight. That is against the law.

"They actually have a law on the books: a Palestinian from Gaza or the West Bank is forbidden to be inside Israel from one to three o'clock in the morning. If I am sleeping in a Tel Aviv bed at that time, I've committed a crime. At that hour, they want Tel Aviv to be 'pure' Jewish.

"However," he continues, "since many Jewish employers find it inconvenient to send all the Arab workers back to Gaza or the West Bank every night, they have silently agreed to allow, or at least have begun the practice of allowing, us to stay overnight. This is a convenience for Israeli employers, since their work force is in place the next morning. There was another silent agreement: if we stayed the night we were to be locked up. By locking us up, out of sight, the police and other Israelis need never know that West Bank Palestinians had defiled their all-Jewish city with our presence.

"I grew accustomed to being locked up when we worked late at the Tel Aviv mattress factory. The plant manager herded us like so many sheep into a warehouse. He shut and secured the steel doors, locking them from the outside. He claimed this was 'protection' for us. One night, however, a fire broke out. All of us tried to climb the walls, but we were trapped, like animals. Firemen eventually broke through the locked doors, but the warehouse was burned to the ground. I suffered horrible burns all over my body and was unable to work for six months. Three other Palestinian workers, all good friends, were burned to death."

Many conditions of plants where he has worked have been hazardous, he claims, "and they are never checked by anyone. Yet we Arabs dare not speak of bad conditions to an employer. We would be fired on the spot."

Many Israeli employers talk frankly about their ambivalence in seeing tens of thousands of Arab workers move each day into their Jewish state. "You have big families," one Jewish boss told Zayid, adding, "We fear that one day you will outnumber us." This boss also frankly told Zayid he was against attempting to annex the West Bank and Gaza "for then we could no longer be a Jewish state."

As the boss talks, Zayid stays quiet. "He may like to express his opinion, but he does it as he would talk to a wall. He is not seeing me, and he would not like me to respond.

"Once a Jewish boss told me, 'I respect you and I suspect you.' In this factory I worked alongside Arabs and Jews, and I never heard the Jewish boss say that to any Jewish worker. Later, someone in this factory stole money from a cashbox. And the Jewish owner did not question the Jewish employees—only me and the other Arabs. They did not find the lost money. But it is a bad psychological treatment they give us. They believe themselves, the Jews, to be better people."

At present, Zayid is a construction worker in a housing unit in Tel Aviv. "The Jews don't want to do construction work. Arabs do most of the construction work in Israel today," Zayid claims.

"We work harder," Zayid boasts, a boast I repeatedly heard made by illegal Mexican immigrants in the United States.

Many Israeli employers say they prefer Arab Palestinians to Jewish workers, and they say this for the same reasons that many United States white employers prefer undocumented Mexicans to legal, unionized workers. The wetbacks, they say, arrive on time, work hard, and never complain. In Israel I heard many of the same comments about Palestinians. "The Arab arrives on time, he works hard, you can pay him about twenty dollars a week, and he never complains. He will take some bread, buy some olives, grab a tomato, and that's his food."

Like the wetback, Zayid has no union to back him up. It's not that there aren't plenty of unions around, but for one reason or another he is barred from their benefits. First, the West Bank Palestinians have organized a couple dozen labor unions, but the Israelis have forbidden these unions to represent the eighty-five thousand laborers who commute each day from Gaza and the West Bank to work for Israeli firms. So why, I ask, doesn't he join the Israeli General Federation of Workers, called the Histadrut?

"I am not permitted to do so," Zayid replies. "No Palestinian worker from Gaza or the West Bank can join."

The Histadrut, Zayid adds, is "a fascinating organization. It is a union, representing all the Israeli workers—and it is also an employer, one of the biggest.

"It owns in whole or in part about fifty of the top two hundred Israeli corporations, and also has extensive interests in South Africa through the Histadrut-controlled Koor Industries. And, as an employer, it wants to make money. And how does one do that in Israel? By hiring cheap Arab labor.

"As an example, I have an Arab friend who works for the Hish-uclei ha-Karmel factory owned by the Histadrut. Most of the workers are Arabs, and once some Israelis complained, saying why did their union hire Arabs when Jews needed jobs. And so the management explained to the Israelis that the heat in the plant was terrible and there were deafening noises and that these were 'black jobs,' 'hard and dirty' work that no Israeli would want to do. So, the Histadrut succeeds in increasing the profits of a company it owns by employing nonunion Arab labor."

Zayid sees hope in the trade unions organized on the West Bank, even if at present they cannot represent Arab workers within Israel. Besides the twenty-four unions in the West Bank with permits to operate, others based in Nablus, Hebron, and Abu Dis in 1981 awaited permission to organize.

"The Israeli military authorities say they must delay their permits until they investigate the membership and leadership. The Israelis will recognize only union leaders who are acceptable to the military authorities because of 'security' considerations. But West Bankers see these security arguments as a pretext for suppressing and controlling political opposition to the military government.

"Arabs who organize West Bank unions risk their lives," Zayid asserts. "The Israelis do not want any leaders to develop. As an example, the Israeli police, with no warning or explanation, went to the home of George Hasboun, deputy general secretary of the West Bank trade unions. They arrested him, handcuffed him, and put him in prison. They kept him there for one year and never filed any charges against him.

"The Israelis also arrested Hassan Baghouti, chairman of the Hotel and Restaurant Workers' Union. They held him in prison in 1978 and never filed charges against him."

The Palestinian union leaders, he says, are operating in alliances with other associations representing engineers, doctors, lawyers, and traders, as well as with various political figures in Gaza and the West

Bank, including the mayors. He adds that in the 1976 municipal elections, several trade-union figures ran in the pro-PLO nationalist lists, and some of them, such as George Hasboun and the deputy mayor of Bethlehem, are municipal leaders as well as union leaders.

There is also now a national Guidance Council for the West Bank and Gaza that coordinates all political activities directed against the occupation. Representatives of the unions, municipalities, and professional associations work together to formulate policies under a pro-PLO banner.

"We are only beginning to learn to speak for ourselves," Zayid concludes.

Later I talk with an Israeli official of the Histadrut, who says, "The West Bank unions are being organized for future elections and they do not do a good job of representing interests of their members on such issues as conditions of work, pay, and other activities normally associated with trade unions." As for the eighty-five thousand West Bank and Gaza Arab workers in Israel—more than thirty percent of the Palestinian work force—who are without trade union representation, he admits that the Histadrut faces a difficulty.

He points out that if the Histadrut makes them full members "the attempt to integrate them might smack of annexation." He also mentions that, owing to bad economic conditions in Israel, some fifty thousand Arab workers may be dismissed. And if that happens, the Israeli treasury could not provide jobs on that scale.

Meanwhile, many Palestinians call Zayid "a traitor" for working in the Jewish state. But one talented Palestinian novelist, Sahar Khalifa, does not see it that way. "One day I decided to write a novel and reconstruct the circumstances that drive the Palestinians to work for the Jews. First, I looked into the economic situation as a whole, in Israel and in Gaza and the West Bank.

"Before I began writing on Palestinian workers I thought that the hero could overcome his circumstances and build his life accordingly," she relates. "I soon realized that there are no heroes in this time and place. There is no way for a Palestinian to achieve anything by himself. Today heroism is that of the group."

As she speaks, I think of Zayid. There is little or no way for him to achieve anything by himself. If he chose to live only for himself, he could perhaps have moved out of the camp and forgotten his

Abdul and Stories of Torture

In the United States, before I went to live in the West Bank, I had heard little about the question of torture of Palestinians by Israelis. Once there, however, after living in Palestinian homes and meeting a variety of Palestinians—merchants, doctors, firemen, students—I soon discovered that in almost any group of, say, five male Palestinians, one would tell me that he had been imprisoned and tortured by Israelis.

I first began to hear about torture of Palestinians when I talked with officials at Bethlehem University and Bir Zeit University. Officials agreed that as many as one-third to one-half the male students had been imprisoned at one time. "And they are tortured," Brother Lowenstein of Bethlehem University told me. "They come back home and they have broken arms or legs. You see their bruises and you know they have been beaten."

Nahla's brother Abdul was one of these. This chapter is largely about Abdul, as well as some two hundred others like him, who talked to me about their time in Israeli jails.

Abdul is one of sixty thousand West Bank and Gaza Palestinians who have been put in Israeli jails since the occupation of these territories began. After Abdul and others told me their stories, I searched for the official "facts" dealing with torture. Allegations of torture have been persistent for more than a decade, ever since the first weeks of the Israeli occupation of the West Bank and Gaza strip after the war of 1967. Israel has consistently said it does not torture Palestinians. I talked with several top Israeli officials and they all insisted that stories of torture were not true. I met one official, however, who, after insisting I must not use his name, said, "Let me remind you that Israel is a Jewish state, determined to remain so. Yet

179

we rule 1.7 million Arabs, and for more than a decade 1.2 million of these have been under military occupation. Under our military rules, we can arrest and hold prisoners without permitting them to see a lawyer. Nor are we required to hold any court proceedings. Under these conditions, in which we report only to ourselves, are you surprised to hear that there is torture? How else do you suppose we keep more than a million people subdued, if not by torture?"

The International Red Cross may visit prisons by appointment only, and, contrary to Israeli claims, they have not given the prisons a clean bill of health. A prisoner, such as Abdul, cannot complain directly to the Red Cross. He must first lodge his complaint with an Israeli prison official, and then be granted permission to talk to a Red Cross representative. The Red Cross has filed repeated complaints about conditions of Israeli prisons and the treatment of Palestinians within these prisons, but Red Cross complaints are filed with the affected government only, in this case the Israelis. Many requests have been made to the Israelis that they release these findings, either publicly or privately, to an impartial international group. But the Israelis refuse to do so.

Amnesty International is the second most important world organization that investigates such matters as torture of political prisoners. Amnesty International reported that Israelis tortured Palestinians, and in 1980, called on the Israeli government "to set up a public and impartial inquiry into complaints of brutality." The international human rights organization urged the Israeli government "to change its procedures immediately" to bar the torture of Palestinians. "The Israeli authorities have not been able to refute persistent complaints of brutality," Amnesty International said.

The London *Sunday Times* conducted extensive research on the subject of torture of Palestinians. A team of reporters, after several weeks of investigation, revealed that "torture of Arab prisoners is so widespread and systematic that it cannot be dismissed as 'rogue cops' exceeding orders. It appears to be deliberate policy."

In Jerusalem, I also talk with an Israeli attorney, Felicia Langer, who has represented hundreds of Palestinians she feels are being held as—and tortured as—political prisoners.

Langer, who studied at Jerusalem's Hebrew University, believes that "the Israeli military courts collude in and knowingly conceal the use of torture by Israel's intelligence and security services. Most convictions are based on so-called confessions by the accused. And I am convinced most of these confessions are extracted by torture."

Many prisoners are held without charges, as "administrative detainees." Attorney Langer says that her efforts to help such Palestinian detainees are usually hopeless.

"There is no legal procedure that deals with administrative detainees. The Israeli authorities are not required by law to give any reason or cause for their detention. They have an appeals committee for administrative detention, but it has no power other than 'to consult.'"

I met several Palestinians who had been arrested and held in jails for several years as administrative detainees. One was Bir Zeit Economics Professor Ghassan Harb. He is of medium build, in his late forties, and speaks in a well-modulated voice. We sit in his office, and he relates this story. The time is April 21, 1974.

"Shortly after midnight, my wife and I are awakened by a half-dozen Israeli soldiers and two men in civilian clothes. They enter my home and order me to get dressed. I ask, 'What is the matter?' and one says, 'You will find out.'"

They handcuff and blindfold Harb and force him to lie down in the back of a jeep. After a journey of two or three hours, the jeep stops. Harb gets out, still blindfolded, and the soldiers place a heavy cloth bag over his head. He is taken into a room, the sack and the blindfold removed, and a man in civilian clothes asks, in Arabic:

"Do you know where you are?"

"No," Harb replies.

"You are in Kasr el-Nihaye."

This is the name of a prison in Baghdad, the capital of Iraq, notorious for its tortures and secret executions. Harb knew he was not in Iraq. But he also knew what Kasr el-Nihaye means: the Palace of the End. And he knew what his interrogator meant.

For two and a half years Harb is held in Israeli prisons without trial. No charges are ever filed; no court case ever held.

"I was sent to a military prison for interrogation. I was beaten, I was tortured," the professor recalls in a calm, detached voice.

"The interrogator would beat me with his fists. Others used sticks and rods to beat my legs and back. I was questioned, beaten, returned to a cell. I was prevented from going outside the cell for exercise or air. I stayed for weeks without being exposed to the sun. My feet and hands were handcuffed all the time I was held in the cell. They used to take me out in some courtyard and drag me naked on the gravel.

"I was beaten by five or six persons. I do not know how many because I was blindfolded, but I could estimate the number by hearing their voices. One kicking, one beating with his fists, another with his leg. Then two would play with me as a ball, one sending me to the other."

As part of the psychological torture used against him, the professor was forced to crawl on all fours and act like a dog. "I was forced to crawl into a kennel for a dog. It was less than two feet square, and I could hear a dog howling nearby."

One Israeli interrogator, if not several, especially liked this form of punishment, and the story of prisoners having to crawl about on all fours became generally known. As a result, one Israeli investigator was demoted and rebuked. In making the announcement, however, the Shin Bet, Israel's security service, insisted that forcing a man to act like a dog was not common practice and used the occasion to insist that "brutality is not practiced."

"The degree of torture or mistreatment differs from one case to another, but all prisoners go through graduated levels of torture, beginning with the beatings," Harb tells me.

And, I ask, during this period is anyone permitted to see the prisoner?

"No one is permitted. Not even a lawyer. They are trying to get a confession of a so-called military involvement or resistance to the Israeli authorities.

"They feel they need the confession because they do not want to tell the truth: that they are arresting persons because of their political views. It would be very difficult for them to justify their actions. They say that in Israel they have democracy. That one can express political ideas. So it would be embarrassing for them to send people to jail for political ideas.

"Therefore they accused me of 'armed' activities. If I had signed a confession that I had engaged in terrorist activity, this would justify—in the view of outsiders—my arrest," Harb points out. "The 'confession' in Hebrew is almost always the sole evidence in a military trial. But I did not admit being involved in the armed struggle against Israel. That was false."

Harb says he worked on the Arab newspaper *Al-Fajr*, published in Jerusalem. He wrote and spoke against the Israeli occupation. "My stories may have irritated the Israelis, but they were not illegal."

Harb's West Bank friends raised the issue of his being held without trial before the United Nations. They said he was being held as a political prisoner.

Israel's ambassador to the United Nations, Jacob Doron, replied, "Nobody is in prison because of political beliefs."

Contrary to the claim of Ambassador Doron, Harb tells me quite simply, "I was arrested, imprisoned, beaten, and tortured because of my political beliefs."

During my first visit with Nablus Mayor Bassam Shaka, he had suggested that I talk with the mother and the wife of a Palestinian, Nader al Afloury, who, he said, "is dying in an Israeli jail from the beatings given him." I go to the home of Nader al Afloury on the outskirts of Nablus. I find a stone home set on a hill, where I meet Nader's wife and mother, who motion me to a chair while they seat themselves on the side of a bed. "They came here at midnight to get him," the mother begins. "They surrounded the house. They were armed soldiers. They handcuffed him and dragged him away. Then others came. They searched the house but did not find anything against him.

"When they took him he was a healthy man. He was twenty-seven, a construction worker. He enjoyed building, working with his hands. Now he has been beaten senseless. He is paralyzed. He cannot speak, nor care for his bodily needs. His fellow prisoners bathe him and feed him."

The mother's eyes—eyes that no longer weep—are wide and stare unblinkingly at me. She is an out-of-shape woman, a vast lump of agony. She has fourteen children—seven girls and seven boys—but having thirteen others does not make the agony of the lost one go away.

"He went insane during interrogation," Nader's wife, twenty-three, tells me. She holds a baby girl her husband has never seen. Her eyes fill with tears. "I went to see him two months after his arrest. Seeing him, I was terrified. He was horribly changed. He no longer responds. He is blind. He weighs no more than eighty pounds.

"We know he is dying," his wife continues. "Now our only hope is that he might be permitted to die at home."

Through a window I see a man riding a donkey, ascending the hill on which the house sits. He ties the donkey, climbs the steps, and enters the room. He is Nader's brother, twenty-five, also a construction worker. We are introduced, and he stays silent. He also has been in prison with no charges filed against him. He too had a child born while he was behind bars.

As Nader's wife serves small cups of Arab coffee, I take a few notes. I tell the mother that to protect the family I need not use the name of her son.

"No, use it," she says. "He is dying. And we cannot save him. If you tell the story of my son, you may help others."

Attorney Langer documents several cases of Palestinian prisoners dying in Israeli jails. "Each Palestinian prisoner's death raises a storm in the Israeli parliament," she reports, "but they do not insist that the jails be opened for general inspection."

She cites the example of a young Palestinian named Qasim Abu Aqr, who lived in Beit-Hanina. "I talked with his cellmates who said Israeli guards returned him to his cell unconscious and blue from beatings. Once after such beatings he did not regain consciousness and died. The interrogators said he had died 'from a fall.' His cellmates said: 'We know his interrogators and we know how he died.'

"Arresting Palestinians and torturing them is a big operation," Langer says. "All of Israel's security services are involved, the Shin Bet, the security service that reports to the Prime Minister; the Military Intelligence, which reports to the Minister of Defense; and the border police and Latam, Israel's 'Department for Special Missions,' both of which report to the police minister."

Several Palestinian women have testified that they were stripped naked and tormented by varying degrees of assault. Aisha Audi, arrested at seventeen, spent ten years in an Israeli prison. The case of Aisha's cousin, Rasmiyyah Audi, was cited in an Amnesty International report in 1979. She reported that Israeli soldiers ripped off her clothes, tied her hands behind her back, and stood around her, "poking my vagina with a stick." After so abusing her, and while she was still naked, they brought in her father, ordering him to take off his clothes and "have sexual intercourse with me." On hearing the words and seeing his daughter so humiliated, her father passed out. "He just collapsed," she testified.

Some months after I first lived with Nahla and her family, I return for a visit and find there is great rejoicing: Abdul has been released from prison. The family is happy, but also sad, for in greeting son and brother they learn he has lost the sight in his left eye. When I see Abdul, the phrase "only skin and bones" comes to mind. Abdul is more bones than skin; everyone says he has lost a great deal of weight during his five years behind bars. He was arrested at seventeen.

"He never knew why he was arrested or imprisoned," Nahla said. "He was never able to talk to a lawyer. The Israelis never filed charges against him. He never had a trial."

Abdul is about five feet, four inches tall. He is nervous and speaks in such a low voice that I must strain to hear. He smokes too much, has lost some of his hair, and looks about thirty-six rather than his actual age of twenty-two.

Abdul has found work in a mechanic's shop in Ramallah, and once, after I visit the shop, he takes a break from work to accompany me to a small cafe for coffee. He worries about his brother Salah, twenty-one, who is held at Nafha prison in the Negev desert. To protest conditions, Palestinian prisoners there went on a hunger strike. Israelis force fed them, and as a result two Palestinian prisoners died. Mordechai Sherman, an Israeli physician at the Nafha prison, admitted the conditions were unfit for human beings.

"My arrest came at the end of Ramadan in 1974," Abdul recalls. "It was about midnight and we were all sleeping. We heard a loud knocking and my parents opened the door. Four heavily armed Israeli soldiers stormed into the house and came to where I was sleeping, hitting me and telling me to get up. I said, 'Let me wash my face,' and they said, 'No, you don't have time.'

"Mother is screaming and holding on to me and my father is asking, What are the charges? And they do not listen, they place handcuffs on me, and then cover my head with a black sack—all of this in front of my parents and Nahla and the others, who are terrified.

"Outside, unable to see, I stumble and fall, face down, and one of the soldiers places a heavy boot on my back, stepping on me, and the other laughs, and then they jerk me up and shove me into a jeep."

Abdul maintains to this day that he does not know why they came for him. "Riding in the jeep that night I tried to think what they would claim I did, to what organization they would insist I belonged—all political organizations for Palestinians being illegal— or if they would insist I had information to incriminate certain friends."

Abdul sat in the back of the jeep as thousands of other Palestinians, including mayors and other dignitaries, have sat. Like them, he was blindfolded, his head covered by a heavy black hood.

"They cover your head and eyes to intimidate you, to keep you in the dark, guessing, wondering, fearful."

The jeep leaves a main highway and goes over bumpy roads and seems to go "in circles" for two or three hours. Perhaps, he now thinks, they were looking for other prisoners. Then the jeep stops abruptly. "The soldiers push me out and through a door and, once inside a prison, they remove the hood and blindfold. An Israeli seated behind a desk questions me in Arabic: What is my name and what is my age and where was I born. When I say, 'Palestine,' the Israeli says, 'There is no Palestine! Where were you born?' Then I answer, 'Ramallah.' After more questions they register me into the prison, which in time I learn is in Nablus."

A visitor traveling north from Jerusalem into Nablus sees this dull, gray, forbidding structure that was built not for men but for beasts, the Turks having used it as a stable for horses and mules one hundred fifty years ago during the Ottoman Empire. It covers a city block and is one of four prisons where Abdul, after being registered that predawn morning of 1974, will sit, stand, wait, and suffer for the next five years of his life. And when Abdul returns to his home his eldest brother Zayid, the construction worker, who is tall and robust, will say the Israelis stunted his brother's growth, that they took his brother as a youth when his bones were not yet fully developed and that, because he did not have a proper diet or proper exercise, Abdul stopped growing and now can never reach the physical strength and capacity he might otherwise have attained.

Abdul talks of unspeakable sanitary conditions—one hundred

men crowded in one small room with one overflowing toilet. The prisoners suffered from intestinal disorders, liver, kidney, and heart disease, and massive infections, with a high percentage of them succumbing to tuberculosis "that usually goes untreated."

Abdul knows the prisons well, having served in four, but he says, "Take Nablus as an example: the walls are thick and damp, and the dampness causes a lot of diseases, such as rheumatism.

"In the dead of winter you cannot imagine what it is to lie down on a concrete floor. I was never provided a bed, not even a mattress. Only blankets thin enough to see through."

Abdul stops to cough. His nagging, persistent cough makes me wonder if he has developed a chronic lung infection from the cold, damp prison.

"Can you imagine, in this small country they maintain fourteen jails for Palestinians," Abdul tells me, listing among the central jails those in Beersheba, Nablus, Ramallah, Hebron, and the so-called Russian compound in Jerusalem, with secondary jails including those in Ramla, Kefar Yonah, Tel-Mond, and Haifa.

There is the danger that Abdul exaggerates, that conditions are not as bad as he paints them for me, but I have no way of checking out the "facts," since reporters have not been permitted to visit the prisons. Once, however, in 1980, after force-fed prisoners in the Nafha prison died, reporters were given a tour of that particular prison. The Israeli press detailed conditions: eight to ten men per cell, no beds, solid steel doors instead of bars, six tiny air holes in the ceiling, insufficient even for light, with food and toilet facilities in the cell itself.

"The outside world cannot know the conditions within the prisons. No one from the outside world goes there, no one but representatives of the Red Cross, and they must call and make an appointment, and they are allowed to see only the prisoners the Israelis want them to see and only the prison sections they are willing to show," Abdul maintains.

"The Red Cross tries, but it can do only so much. A representative comes to visit once a month and brings some food and asks about our treatment, what we need. And once I tell him frankly: the guards treat us bad, and we do not have enough food or light or books. And afterward an interrogator says, 'You are a stupid ant.'

Then they send me to solitary confinement, and they take away my blankets.

"In five years, I received no parcels of food or books from home. The Israelis forbid this.

"A prisoner may have a visitor once a month. And the time of the visit is about fifteen minutes. There is a grille between you and the visitor. You may not touch. And while you are visiting, the soldiers are by your side, listening, so you cannot tell your visitor—usually it is your mother or your father—what is going on inside the jail nor learn what is happening outside. You are not allowed to talk freely. You ask how they are feeling, or who has gotten married—these are the only matters you are allowed to discuss."

Twice in five years Abdul got letters, one from his mother and one from Nahla. "Every letter is censored, so I told them not to write."

Nahla has told me that Abdul was "beaten and tortured"—that torture of Palestinians is common practice in Israeli jails.

"I do not like to remember the beatings, the torturing," Abdul says. "Because it is difficult for a person to go on remembering such horrible experiences. But I am thinking of my brother Salah, who is still in prison. I know he is suffering, and I think my story might help stop the brutality against Palestinians.

"The Israelis use three levels of torture," he continues. "The first includes beatings with fists, sticks, and rods on the legs, arms, back, and head."

Initially, he recalls, he is seated in a room before three interrogators. "One is a European Jew from Germany or Poland, I think, but he likes to use an Arab nickname, and he is called Zaki—Captain Zaki. He is tall and fair-haired and thin. He says he is my friend, and that I should confess. And he hands me a typed sheet, in Hebrew, and asks me to sign it. And I say I do not read Hebrew and would not sign it. Then one of the others, a Syrian Jew whose name was Abu Ali, begins to hit me. He uses his fists on my face and on my stomach."

In this first level, which includes "simple beatings," as Abdul calls them, he is swung like a Yo-Yo from Captain Zaki to Abu Ali, who, Abdul says, has a definite job classification: to beat prisoners. "He and others do nothing else but this. They sometimes chew gum and even whistle as they beat you, and once Abu Ali says, 'Even if you want to confess, do not tell me. My job is only to beat you.'"

Once, as he pummels Abdul in the stomach, Abu Ali says, "I hate you," and he relates that "In Syria Arabs killed my brother. And now I get my revenge." Another Israeli guard, an Iraqi Jew who beat Abdul with a rod, tells him, "I hate you and all you dirty Arabs."

"I learned that this man's brother was killed some years previously by a bomb planted by Palestinians," Abdul says. He is sent to what he calls a dungeon, where he cannot wash his body or see daylight.

Again taken before interrogators, Abdul maintains he does not know the cause of his arrest, and if they have any evidence against him they should reveal it. "At this moment they start hitting me again. Two soldiers and one civilian investigator. They use rods and hit me continuously for about one hour, concentrating on the muscles of my left hand." The interrogator asks him about Fatah, one of the organizations within the PLO that is led by Yasser Arafat.

"I say that I am not involved in any illegal organization. They do not believe my words. They order me to undress. Two soldiers pour hot water over me, then cold, then hot. I am forced to lie on the floor. One stands on my legs. Another pulls my arms back. And they say, 'You must tell us you are in this illegal organization.' I deny this.

"They return me again for such beatings. On this occasion, they concentrate on my face, near my left eye. Afterward the eye has a bleeding, and I lose sight in that eye."

Abdul does not have the eye covered, and it wanders at will and occasionally fixes a blank stare at me. I try to concentrate on his right eye.

After the beatings, Abdul "graduates" to a more sophisticated type of punishment, a type that is even more difficult to bear but does not leave telltale marks of battered and sightless eyes and broken bones. The body is often permanently damaged from this, but the damage is more internal than external.

Abdul gives, as an example, his being strung up on a wall, "like a slab of beef." He and others are left dangling, and eventually, depending, he leads me to believe, on the whim or inclination of a guard, he is lifted off a hook and taken away to the interrogators. Depending on whether he is ready or not ready to do their bidding, he is released from that particular punishment or taken back and again strung up for an additional period of dangling. With little blood circulating to his extremities, Abdul says he feared paralysis.

"As I hung there, I constantly wiggled my fingers to keep them alive.

"Always, when strung on a wall, I was blindfolded, handcuffed, and stripped naked. The guards see most of their prisoners most of the time without the prisoners wearing a stitch of clothes. They enjoy our humiliation.

"This second level of torture includes enforced sleeplessness," Abdul continues. "I was in a solitary cell. And they piped in loud, screeching noises and the screams of tortured prisoners. They flooded the cell day and night with strong lights. I did not sleep for three days. Then they called me to the investigators. And I tell them, 'I want to sleep,' and they say 'No. It is forbidden to sleep until you tell us.' As I am standing, my legs buckle and I fall. A soldier kicks me, pulls me on my feet, and says, 'You will talk. Or you will never sleep!'

"I am led off to a kind of box. I am pushed inside. But it is so designed that I cannot sit down nor stand upright and yet must support myself on my feet, in a stooped position."

Once the soldiers have stuffed him inside this box and locked the door, he cries out in pain and lifts one foot and then the other and finds no relief because each time a foot goes down it lands on a floor closely studded with razor-sharp spikes.

"Each is like a needle or a small, sharp nail. They tear into my flesh, and my feet bleed profusely. Then I am taken from this torture chamber and led away, this time to a kind of playpen, where I must walk in mounds of salt."

The psychological torture, Abdul maintains, is worse than the physical.

"Over a period of time I began to believe that I was born into the wrong race of people, that the Jews—those in charge—are right. I have difficulty understanding this, but all around me for five years are those who are powerful, who have voices, who make decisions. They are the Jews. I begin to see myself as they see me, as they identify me. They call me 'ant' and say I am excrement, and I tell myself not to believe it.

"Then I am stripped naked, and they force me to walk on all fours and bark like a dog.

"Soldiers with rods and sticks beat me, and one jumps on and off my back. They force me to crawl into a kennel and sit there and repeat, 'I am a dog.' And the most horrible part is that I begin to see myself as they see me, low and mean and inhuman."

Still maintaining he is innocent of any criminal acts against the state of Israel, Abdul now "graduates" to the third level of torture, which includes the application of electricity in bands placed around his head and also in a chair, in which he is strapped for doses that he says "blow him away."

In the third level there are sexual sadists who, to hear Abdul tell it, do nothing all day but twist and squeeze the genitals of Palestinians, who are naked and strapped to chairs.

Abdul says he was once forced against a wall, his legs apart, and strapped in that position. A specialist in sexual sadism then attached electrical wires to his testicles. Another day he is handcuffed and stripped, pinned to the floor by a guard while an interrogator forces a Coke bottle up his rectum. Other "specialists" push ballpoint refills into prisoners' penises.

"Interrogators try by every means to force you to sign a 'confession,' written in Hebrew, that will be used as evidence in a military trial. With such trials, they try to show they keep only confessed criminals as prisoners.

"The degree of torture differs from one case to another," Abdul continues. "But almost all prisoners go through these stages, beginning with the beatings. One is lucky to get out alive. And no one gets out without some kind of permanent disability—for me it's the loss of an eye. Another will have a permanent loss of a hand or an arm or a leg. You will suffer permanent damage to your stomach or back. You cannot come out 'free.'"

Was he not able to call an attorney? I ask.

"You are not permitted to see anyone during interrogation. Not even a lawyer. They want you to confess to a so-called military involvement or involvement in a military struggle against the authorities. I did not admit that. It would be false. They found no evidence against me. Nevertheless, they held me as an administrative detainee for five years."

Epilogue

The Holy Land has always been only a tiny fragment in the vastness of the universe and yet it has, in ways that we understand and in ways that we do not understand, influenced all of our lives.

From this small spot on earth, long-ago shepherds and fishermen gave us the light as they saw it and phrased their emotions in a way that allows billions of people in one way or another, in one ritual or another, to relate to their visions of brotherhood and sisterhood and peace.

I have seen grander sights than the Holy Land. I have viewed mighty oceans, the majestic Andes and Himalayas, and valleys that are pure delight. In the Holy Land one does not find much that takes one's breath away, not in nature or monuments made by man. One finds nothing to equal the Forum of Rome, the Parthenon of Athens, the Tuileries or the Place de la Concorde in Paris.

Yet, beginning with the earliest shepherds and continuing to this day, men and women have idealized the Holy Land and turned it into "a symbol and an allegory" rather than a place. I crossed the Jordan, muddy and narrow enough to throw a stone across. Yet for millions of faithful it remains a mystic boundary over which their dead have gone into the Promised Land. The Galilee is in fact a lovely lake. Yet for millions it long ago ceased to be geography and has become romance, the place where Christ walked on the water.

Jerusalem is the celestial city that comes "down out of heaven from God." The visitor or resident may think Jerusalem means Paradise, the celestial place, and so he says, Here I am in Paradise—and never mind the greed, the man with the sores, the bomb that just went off, or the soldier with the submachine gun. One sees what he or she brings within, the actual geography turning into allegories, the stories one has heard and accepted as "truth."

When I was growing up, "place" was important. Many Christians believed that to touch the ground where Jesus trod would make one a better Christian. "Place" still remains important to millions of Jews, Christians, and Muslims, who fight the unholiest of wars over the holiest of ground. Yet true religion is not a desire for place but a desire for God.

In living with persons of three faiths—Judaism, Christianity, and Islam—I found the similarities of religions striking. The founders all came from one small area of the world in western Asia; they were all a Semitic people. Each religion is monotheistic, with a belief in one Supreme Being. Each claims a specified revealed truth: that you can obtain supreme satisfaction by obedience to God.

Each claims an inspired Scripture. Each recognizes a sacred community—a particular group of people regarded as peculiarly sacred. Each has some kind of belief that one should treat others as he wants to be treated. Each has hopes and fears of a future life. Each expresses most fundamentally a desire for God.

A desire for God takes one ultimately, I believe, to a universalism. A universalism grants the assumption that any great world religion has enough good within it to provide guidelines for all men and women to live in peace. The fact that we do not have peace is a deficiency, not in the religions, but in us, far-from-perfect creatures that we are.

Being a "good" Jew, Christian, or Muslim, I think, is to recognize our failings. It is to view ourselves as a part of all that has gone before. I like especially what the philosopher Maimonides said: that he gained the most knowledge about God by looking at the stars.

I always was aware of the stars over Jerusalem, Bethlehem, over the refugee camps, and over the Jewish settlements on the West Bank.

Perhaps these same stars that inspired Moses and Christ and Muhammad in their desert homes will inspire new leaders who will embrace one another with confidence, faith, and trust, saying, We are truly one people.